JOHN
for
EVERYONE

PART 1
CHAPTERS 1–10

20TH ANNIVERSARY EDITION WITH STUDY GUIDE

NEW TESTAMENT FOR EVERYONE
20TH ANNIVERSARY EDITION WITH STUDY GUIDE
N. T. Wright

Matthew for Everyone, Part 1
Matthew for Everyone, Part 2
Mark for Everyone
Luke for Everyone
John for Everyone, Part 1
John for Everyone, Part 2
Acts for Everyone, Part 1
Acts for Everyone, Part 2
Romans for Everyone, Part 1
Romans for Everyone, Part 2
1 Corinthians for Everyone
2 Corinthians for Everyone
Galatians and Thessalonians for Everyone
Ephesians, Philippians, Colossians and Philemon for Everyone
1 and 2 Timothy and Titus for Everyone
Hebrews for Everyone
James, Peter, John and Judah for Everyone
Revelation for Everyone

JOHN

for

EVERYONE

PART 1
CHAPTERS 1–10

20TH ANNIVERSARY EDITION WITH STUDY GUIDE

N. T.
WRIGHT

STUDY GUIDE BY SALLY D. SHARPE

WESTMINSTER
JOHN KNOX PRESS
LOUISVILLE • KENTUCKY

© 2002, 2004, 2023 Nicholas Thomas Wright
Study guide © 2023 Westminster John Knox Press

First published in Great Britain in 2002 by the
Society for Promoting Christian Knowledge
36 Causton Street
London SW1P 4ST
www.spckpublishing.co.uk

Copublished in 2004 by the Society for Promoting
Christian Knowledge, London, and Westminster John Knox Press,
100 Witherspoon Street, Louisville, KY 40202.

20th Anniversary Edition with Study Guide
Published in 2023
by Westminster John Knox Press
Louisville, Kentucky

23 24 25 26 27 28 29 30 31 32 – 10 9 8 7 6 5 4 3 2 1

Cover design by Allison Taylor

Library of Congress Cataloging-in-Publication Data is on file at the Library of Congress, Washington, DC.

ISBN-13: 978-0-664-26640-0

Most Westminster John Knox Press books are available at special quantity discounts when purchased in bulk by corporations, organizations and special-interest groups. For more information, please e-mail SpecialSales@wjkbooks.com.

For
Oliver,
remembering John's words
about the father and the son

CONTENTS

CONTENTS

INTRODUCTION TO THE
ANNIVERSARY EDITION

It took me ten years, but I'm glad I did it. Writing a guide to the books of the New Testament felt at times like trying to climb all the Scottish mountains in quick succession. But the views from the tops were amazing, and discovering new pathways up and down was very rewarding as well. The real reward, though, has come in the messages I've received from around the world, telling me that the books have been helpful and encouraging, opening up new and unexpected vistas.

Perhaps I should say that this series wasn't designed to help with sermon preparation, though many preachers have confessed to me that they've used it that way. The books were meant, as their title suggests, for everyone, particularly for people who would never dream of picking up an academic commentary but who nevertheless want to dig a little deeper.

The New Testament seems intended to provoke all readers, at whatever stage, to fresh thought, understanding and practice. For that, we all need explanation, advice and encouragement. I'm glad these books seem to have had that effect, and I'm delighted that they are now available with study guides in these new editions.

N. T. Wright
2022

INTRODUCTION

On the very first occasion when someone stood up in public to tell people about Jesus, he made it very clear: this message is for *everyone*.

It was a great day – sometimes called the birthday of the church. The great wind of God's spirit had swept through Jesus' followers and filled them with a new joy and a sense of God's presence and power. Their leader, Peter, who only a few weeks before had been crying like a baby because he'd lied and cursed and denied even knowing Jesus, found himself on his feet explaining to a huge crowd that something had happened which had changed the world for ever. What God had done for him, Peter, he was beginning to do for the whole world: new life, forgiveness, new hope and power were opening up like spring flowers after a long winter. A new age had begun in which the living God was going to do new things in the world – beginning then and there with the individuals who were listening to him. 'This promise is for *you*,' he said, 'and for your children, and for everyone who is far away' (Acts 2.39). It wasn't just for the person standing next to you. It was for everyone.

Within a remarkably short time this came true to such an extent that the young movement spread throughout much of the known world. And one way in which the *everyone* promise worked out was through the writings of the early Christian leaders. These short works – mostly letters and stories about Jesus – were widely circulated and eagerly read. They were never intended for either a religious or intellectual elite. From the very beginning they were meant for everyone.

That is as true today as it was then. Of course, it matters that some people give time and care to the historical evidence, the meaning of the original words (the early Christians wrote in Greek), and the exact and particular force of what different writers were saying about God, Jesus, the world and themselves. This series is based quite closely on that sort of work. But the point of it all is that the message can get out to everyone, especially to people who wouldn't normally read a book with footnotes and Greek words in it. That's the sort of person for whom these books are written. And that's why there's a glossary, in the back, of the key words that you can't really get along without, with a simple description of what they mean. Whenever you see a word in **bold type** in the text, you can go to the back and remind yourself what's going on.

There are of course many translations of the New Testament available today. The one I offer here is designed for the same kind of reader: one who mightn't necessarily understand the more formal, sometimes even ponderous, tones of some of the standard ones. I have of course tried to keep as close to the original as I can. But my main aim has been to be sure that the words can speak not just to some people, but to everyone.

Let me add a note about the translation the reader will find here of the Greek word *Christos*. Most translations simply say 'Christ', but most modern English speakers assume that that word is simply a proper name (as though 'Jesus' were Jesus 'Christian' name and 'Christ' were his 'surname'). For all sorts of reasons, I disagree; so I have experimented not only with 'Messiah' (which is what the word literally means) but sometimes, too, with 'King'.

The gospel of John has always been a favourite for many. At one level it is the simplest of all the gospels; at another level it is the most profound. It gives the appearance of being written by someone who was a very close friend of Jesus, and who spent the rest of his life mulling over, more and more deeply, what Jesus had done and said and achieved, praying it through from every angle, and helping others to understand it. Countless people down the centuries have found that, through reading this gospel, the figure of Jesus becomes real for them, full of warmth and light and promise. It is, in fact, one of the great books in the literature of the world; and part of its greatness is the way it reveals its secrets not just to high-flown learning, but to those who come to it with humility and hope. So here it is: John for everyone!

Tom Wright

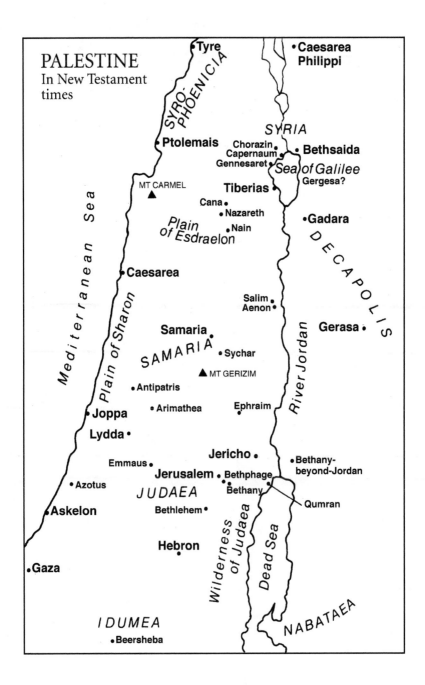

PALESTINE
In New Testament times

Tyre

Caesarea Philippi

SYRO-PHOENICIA

SYRIA

Ptolemais

Chorazin
Capernaum
Gennesaret
Bethsaida

Sea of Galilee

Gergesa?

MT CARMEL

Tiberias

Cana

Nazareth

Gadara

Nain

DECAPOLIS

Plain of Esdraelon

Mediterranean Sea

Caesarea

Salim
Aenon

Plain of Sharon

Samaria

Gerasa

SAMARIA

Sychar

River Jordan

MT GERIZIM

Antipatris

Arimathea

Ephraim

Joppa

Lydda

Jericho

Emmaus

Bethany-beyond-Jordan

Jerusalem

Bethphage

Azotus

Bethany

JUDAEA

Qumran

Askelon

Bethlehem

Wilderness of Judaea

Dead Sea

Hebron

Gaza

IDUMEA

NABATAEA

Beersheba

JOHN 1.1–18

The Word Made Flesh

¹In the beginning was the Word. The Word was close beside God, and the Word was God. ²In the beginning, he was close beside God.

³All things came into existence through him; not one thing that exists came into existence without him. ⁴Life was in him, and this life was the light of the human race. ⁵The light shines in the darkness, and the darkness did not overcome it.

⁶There was a man called John, who was sent from God. ⁷He came as evidence, to give evidence about the light, so that everyone might believe through him. ⁸He was not himself the light, but he came to give evidence about the light.

⁹The true light, which gives light to every human being, was coming into the world. ¹⁰He was in the world, and the world was made through him, and the world did not know him. ¹¹He came to what was his own, and his own people did not accept him. ¹²But to anyone who did accept him, he gave the right to become God's children; yes, to anyone who believed in his name. ¹³They were not born from blood, or from fleshly desire, or from the intention of a man, but from God.

¹⁴And the Word became flesh, and lived among us. We gazed upon his glory, glory like that of the father's only son, full of grace and truth. ¹⁵John gave evidence about him, loud and clear.

'This is the one', he said, 'that I was speaking about when I told you, "The one who comes after me ranks ahead of me, because he was before me."'

¹⁶Yes; it's out of his fullness that we have all received, grace indeed on top of grace. ¹⁷The law, you see, was given through Moses; grace and truth came through Jesus the Messiah. ¹⁸Nobody has ever seen God. The only-begotten God, who is intimately close to the father – he has brought him to light.

'It's on the right just beyond the end of the village,' my friend had said. 'You'll see where to turn – it's got the name on the gate.'

It sounded straightforward. Here was the village. I drove slowly past the pretty cottages, the small shops and the old church.

To begin with, I thought I must have misheard him. There didn't seem to be any houses just outside the village. But then I came to the gateway. Tall stone pillars, overhanging trees and an old wooden sign with the right name on it. Inside, a wide gravel drive stretching away, round a corner out of sight. There were daffodils on the grass verge either side, in front of the thick rhododendron bushes.

I turned in to the driveway. He never told me he lived somewhere like *this*! I drove round the corner; then round another corner, with more daffodils and bushes. Then, as I came round a final bend, I gasped.

There in front of me was the house. Sheltered behind tall trees, surrounded by lawns and shrubbery, with the morning sunlight picking out the colour in the old stone. And there was my friend, emerging from between the pillars around the front porch, coming to greet me.

Approaching John's **gospel** is a bit like arriving at a grand, imposing house. Many Bible readers know that this gospel is not quite like the others. They may have heard, or begun to discover, that it's got hidden depths of meaning. According to one well-known saying, this book is like a pool that's safe for a child to paddle in but deep enough for an elephant to swim in. But, though it's imposing in its structure and ideas, it's not meant to scare you off. It makes you welcome. Indeed, millions have found that, as they come closer to this book, the Friend above all friends is coming out to meet them.

Like many a grand house, the book has a driveway, bringing you off the main road, telling you something about the place you're getting to before you get there. These opening verses are, in fact, such a complete introduction to the book that by the time you get to the story you know a good deal about what's coming, and what it means. It's almost as though the long driveway contained signs with pictures of the various rooms in the house and the people you were going to meet there. This passage has become famous because it's often read at Christmas carol services – though it isn't just about the birth of Jesus, but about the full meaning of everything he was, and is, and did. And the more we explore the gospel itself, the more we'll discover what a complete introduction to it this short passage is.

The gateway to the drive is formed by the unforgettable opening words: 'In the beginning was the **Word**.' At once we know that we are entering a place which is both familiar and strange. 'In the beginning' – no Bible reader could see that phrase and not think at once of the start of Genesis, the first book in the Old Testament: 'In the beginning God created the heavens and the earth.' Whatever else John is going to tell us, he wants us to see his book as the story of God and the world, not just the story of one character in one place and time. This book is about the creator God acting in a new way within his much-loved creation. It is about the way in which the long story which began in Genesis reached the climax the creator had always intended.

And it will do this through 'the Word'. In Genesis 1, the climax is the creation of humans, made in God's image. In John 1, the climax is the arrival of a human being, the Word become 'flesh'.

When I speak a word, it is, in a sense, part of me. It's a breath that comes from inside me, making the noise that I give it with my throat, my mouth and my tongue. When people hear it, they assume I intended it. 'But you said . . .', people comment, if our deeds don't match up to our words. We remain responsible for the words we say.

And yet our words have a life which seems independent of us. When people hear them, words can change the way they think and live. Think of 'I love you'; or, 'It's time to go'; or, 'You're fired'. These words create new situations. People respond or act accordingly. The words remain in their memory and go on affecting them.

In the Old Testament, God regularly acts by means of his 'word'. What he says, happens – in Genesis itself, and regularly thereafter. 'By the word of the Lord', says the psalm, 'the heavens were made' (33.6). God's word is the one thing that will last, even though people and plants wither and die (Isaiah 40.6–8); God's word will go out of his mouth and bring life, healing and hope to Israel and the whole creation (Isaiah 55.10–11). That's part of what lies behind John's choice of 'Word' here, as a way of telling us who Jesus really is.

John probably expects some readers to see that this opening passage says, about Jesus himself, what some writers had said about 'Wisdom'. Many Jewish teachers had grappled with the age-old questions: How can the one true God be both different from the world and active within the world? How can he be remote, holy and detached, and also intimately present? Some had already spoken of the 'word' and 'wisdom' as ways of answering these questions. Some had already combined them within the belief that the one true God had promised to place his own 'presence' within the **Temple** in Jerusalem. Others saw them enshrined in the Jewish law, the **Torah**. All of this, as we shall see, is present in John's mind when he writes of God's 'Word'.

But the idea of the Word would also make some of his readers think of ideas that pagan philosophers had discussed. Some spoke of the 'word' as a kind of principle of rationality, lying deep within the whole cosmos and within all human beings. Get in touch with this principle, they said, and your life will find its true meaning. Well, maybe, John is saying to them; but the Word isn't an abstract principle, it's a person. And I'm going to introduce you to him.

Verses 1–2 and 18 begin and end the passage by stressing that the Word was and is God, and is intimately close to God. John knows perfectly well he's making language go beyond what's normally possible, but it's Jesus that makes him do it; because verse 14 says that the Word became flesh – that is, became human, became one of us. He became, in fact, the human being we know as Jesus. That's the theme of this gospel: if you want to know who the true God is, look long and hard at Jesus.

The rest of the passage clusters around this central statement. The one we know as Jesus is identical, it seems, with the Word who was there from the very start, the Word through whom all things were made, the one who contained and contains **life** and light. The Word challenged the darkness before creation and now challenges the darkness that is found, tragically, within creation itself. The Word is bringing into being the new creation, in which God says once more, 'Let there be light!'

But when God sends the Word into the world, the world pretends it doesn't recognize him. Indeed, when he sends the Word specifically to Israel, the chosen people don't recognize him. This is the central problem which dominates the whole gospel story. Jesus comes to God's people, and God's people do what the rest of the world do: they prefer darkness to light. That is why fresh grace is needed, on top of the grace already given (verse 16): the **law**, given by Moses, points in the right direction, but, like Moses himself, it doesn't take us to the promised land. For that, you need the grace and truth that come through Jesus the **Messiah**, the **son of God**.

Perhaps the most exciting thing about this opening passage is that we're in it too: 'To anyone who did accept him' (verse 12) – that means anyone at all, then and now. You don't have to be born into a particular family or part of the world. God wants people from everywhere to be born in a new way, born into the family which he began through Jesus and which has since spread through the world. Anyone can become a 'child of God' in this sense, a sense which goes beyond the fact that all humans are special in God's sight. Something can happen to people in this life which causes them to become new people, people who (as verse 12 says) 'believe in his name'. Somehow (John will tell us how, step-by-step, as we go forward into the great building to which this driveway has led us) the great drama of God and the world, of Jesus and Israel, of the Word who reveals the glory of the unseen God – this great drama is a play in search of actors, and there are parts for everyone, you and me included.

As we make our way up this driveway towards the main building, a figure crosses our path. Is this, perhaps, our friend? He turns and looks, but points us on to the house. He isn't the man we want, but his job is to point us to him. He is, in John's language, 'giving evidence about the light'. If we are to meet the Word of God, all four gospels suggest we do well to begin by considering **John the Baptist**.

JOHN 1.19–28

The Evidence of John

[19]This is the evidence John gave, when the Judaeans sent priests and Levites from Jerusalem to ask him, 'Who are you?'

[20]He was quite open about it; he didn't try to deny it. He said, quite openly, 'I am not the Messiah.'

[21]'What then?' they asked. 'Are you Elijah?'

'No, I'm not,' he replied.

'Are you the Prophet?'

'No.'

[22]'Well, then, who *are* you?' they said. 'We've got to take some kind of answer back to the people who sent us. Who do you claim to be?'

[23]'I'm "a voice calling in the desert",' he said, '"Straighten out the road for the master!"' – just as the prophet Isaiah said.

[24]The people who had been sent were from the Pharisees. [25]They continued to question him.

'So why are you baptizing', they asked, 'if you aren't the Messiah, or Elijah, or the Prophet?'

[26]'I'm baptizing with water,' John replied. 'But there is someone standing among you that you don't know, [27]someone who is to come after me. I'm not good enough to undo his sandal-strap.'

[28]This took place in Bethany beyond the Jordan, where John was baptizing.

'I want to make it quite clear that I'm not a candidate.'

You hear that said over and over as politicians jostle for position before a major election. No, they aren't going to stand. No, they have no intention of running for office. No, they are going to sit this one out. And then – surprise, surprise – suddenly they make a speech saying that friends have advised them, that pressure has been put on them, that for the good of the country they now intend . . . to run after all. And we have become quite cynical about it all.

But here we have a story about a man pushing himself forward in the public eye, gaining a large following, and then refusing to claim any of the offices they were eager to ascribe to him. John, the writer of this **gospel**, assumes that we know a certain amount about the 'offices' or leadership characters that many Jews were expecting at the time. The **Messiah**: well, of course. The king from the house of David. The king who would overthrow all injustice and rule over Israel, and perhaps the world too. But **John** denies quite firmly that he is the Messiah, and seems to mean it. He isn't doing messianic things.

But what about Elijah and 'the Prophet'?

For centuries the Jews had read in the Bible that the great prophet, Elijah, would return before the great and terrible 'day of the Lord' (Malachi 4.5). Elijah, it seemed, hadn't died in the ordinary way, but had been taken up to **heaven** directly (2 Kings 2). Now, many believed, he would return to herald God's new day. Indeed, many Christians, and most likely Jesus as well, believed that John was in fact Elijah, even

5

JOHN 1.19–28 The Evidence of John

if he didn't think so – a puzzle to which the New Testament offers no solution (see, e.g., Mark 9.13). But, anyway, John clearly didn't want anyone thinking he was Elijah.

Elijah wasn't the only great prophet. Most in Jesus' day would have ranked him second to Moses himself. In Deuteronomy 18.15–18 God promises that he will raise up a prophet like Moses to lead the people. This figure, a yet-to-come 'prophet like Moses', was expected in Jesus' day (see 6.14), though most people probably didn't distinguish sharply between the different 'figures' they had heard or read about. Enough to know that *someone* would come, and preferably soon, to sort out the mess they were in.

But John refused all such titles. A group of **priests** and Levites – **Temple** functionaries – came to check him out, sent by the **Pharisees** who were one of the leading pressure groups of the time. They had their own reasons for wanting to keep tabs on people. If someone was behaving in a strange new way, announcing a **message** from God, they wanted to know about it. And John was indeed behaving strangely. Israel's scriptures hadn't spoken of a prophet who would come and plunge people into water. Why was he doing it?

John's answer, here and in what follows, is that he is getting people ready for someone else. The one claim he makes – apart from his belief that Israel's God has commanded him to baptize people in water – is that he is a 'voice'. Or rather, *the* voice, the voice spoken of by Isaiah, in the same passage where he speaks of the grass withering but the **Word** of God standing forever (40.1–8). John wants us to make the connection with verses 1–18. And what the voice commands is to get the road straightened out. The master is coming; the way must be prepared.

I live near a busy city street, and several times a day I hear sirens blaring as a police car, or a fire engine, or an ambulance, tries to make its way through heavy traffic to yet another emergency. That's the sort of task John claims to have: sounding his siren to clear a path for the one who's coming behind him. Already, in the Prologue (the great opening section in verses 1–18), we have seen this picture of John: he wasn't the light, but came to give evidence about it (1.8). He is of secondary importance to the Messiah, although he comes before him in temporal sequence. The reason he comes before him, of course, is that he has to, in order to clear the way ahead.

John the Baptist occupies a position like this in all the gospels, and indeed within the early Christian proclamation as a whole. The movement looked back to John as its launch pad. At the same time, there were some groups of John's followers who, for whatever reason, never made the transition to following Jesus. It's possible that the writer, aware of such groups, is wanting to emphasize that John the Baptist insisted that people should follow Jesus, not himself. And he really meant it.

One of the many points to ponder about the strange character of John the Baptist is the way in which all Christian preachers are called to the same attitude that John had. We don't proclaim ourselves, as Paul said, but Jesus the **Messiah** as Lord, and ourselves as your servants for his sake (2 Corinthians 4.5). Or, as John put it, 'I'm only a voice.' There is his humility, and his true greatness.

JOHN 1.29–34

The Lamb and the Spirit

[29]The next day, John saw Jesus coming towards him.

'Look!' he said. 'There's God's lamb! He's the one who takes away the world's sin! [30]He's the one I was speaking about when I said, "There's a man coming after me who ranks ahead of me, because he was before me!" [31]I didn't know who it would be, but this was the reason I came to baptize with water – so that he could be revealed to Israel.'

[32]So John gave this evidence: 'I saw the spirit coming down like a dove out of heaven and remaining on him. [33]I didn't know who it would be; but the one who sent me to baptize with water said to me, "When you see the spirit coming down and resting on someone, that's the person who will baptize with the holy spirit." [34]Well, that's what I saw, and I've given you my evidence: he is the son of God.'

'What I want to know is – what's that sheep doing there?'

The student had been sick for several days, and I went to visit him. He was in his first year at university, and the whole world of cultural and intellectual enquiry was opening up in front of him like an Aladdin's cave. His girlfriend had brought him a history of Western art, to help him pass the time until he was well enough to study again. And for the first time he was thinking about what the paintings meant.

He had come to a painting of **John the Baptist**. For many centuries it was the rule that in the picture, beside John, there would be a lamb. Sometimes John is pointing to it; sometimes it's simply sitting there looking thoughtful. Sometimes the point is made more obvious by blood pouring from its side, perhaps being caught in a chalice. I can't remember which picture it was the student was looking at, but I presume there was simply what looked like a healthy sheep standing beside the great bearded prophet.

I explained. John the Baptist is famous for many things, but the central and most important role he has in the New Testament is to point away from himself and towards Jesus. In particular, here in John's **gospel**, he points him out as 'God's lamb'. And with that he indicates, at the very start of the gospel story, how things are going to end, and why. Jesus is to die a sacrificial death for the sins of the world.

By the end of the story, John (the gospel-writer, not the Baptist) has made the meaning clear. The death of Jesus takes place, in this gospel, on the afternoon when the Passover lambs were being killed in the **Temple**. Jesus is the true Passover lamb. John, like many New Testament writers but in his own particular way, wants us to understand the events concerning Jesus as a new, and better, **Exodus** story. Just as God brought the children of Israel out of Egypt, so God was now bringing a new people out of an even older and darker slavery.

But who is this new people? In the original Exodus story, Israel is rescued from the dark powers of the world, which in that case meant the Egyptians under Pharaoh. But now, according to John, God's lamb is going to take away the sin of the world itself. This can only mean that God's rescue operation is moving out, wider than just Israel, to embrace the whole of creation.

This has already been hinted in the Prologue (1.12–13). *Everybody* who receives the **Word**, who believes in his name, can become a new-born child of God. Everybody – not just those with a particular pedigree or certificate of achievement. Again and again in John's gospel we will see the ancient people of God, not least their rulers and self-appointed guardians of tradition, missing the meaning of what Jesus is doing, while people on the edges, outside the boundaries, get the point and find themselves forgiven, healed, brought in by God's transforming love. This is what we are to understand when John the Baptist points Jesus out as 'God's lamb, taking away the world's sin'.

How did John know this? He tells us himself. It was something that happened at Jesus' **baptism**.

The actual baptism of Jesus isn't described in this gospel (nor, for that matter, is the Last Supper). The writer seems to assume that we know about it. In fact, throughout this first chapter he seems to assume that his readers are already familiar with a certain amount of the story of Jesus. This doesn't necessarily mean that he's writing after the other gospels were written; the stories were well known in the early church long before they reached their present written form. But here, and frequently, John has in mind the larger scene which we know from elsewhere. He doesn't bother repeating it, because he is keen to draw our attention to its meaning.

Here we have the heart of John's 'evidence': Jesus is the one upon whom God's **spirit** comes down and rests. And this means that he is the one who will baptize not just with water, like John, but with the **holy spirit**.

Once again, then, John the Baptist points to one of the key things Jesus has come to do. Like Jesus' death, this will be fulfilled in the last pages of the story. We hear about the spirit intermittently in this gospel, particularly in the remarkable passage 7.37–39, and in the great 'farewell discourses' of chapters 14–16. But it's only in the final scenes that the spirit is given to Jesus' followers. Only when the lamb has been killed for the world's sins can the spirit of the living God be poured out on his people. Only when the Temple has been made clean and ready – the Temple of human hearts, polluted by sin and rebellion – can the presence of God come and live there. So, on the evening of the first Easter Day, Jesus breathes on his **disciples**, giving them his own spirit, his own breath, to be theirs (20.21–23).

When John the Baptist declares, on the basis of this evidence, that Jesus is 'the **son of God**', the first and most obvious meaning this deep and rich phrase would have is 'the **Messiah**'. We, reading the gospel, know there is more to it than that, because the Prologue has already told us that Jesus is 'the only-begotten God' (1.18) – an extraordinary and unique phrase, saying simultaneously that Jesus is one with the father and yet to be distinguished from him. He is, in fact, the Word who was always with God, who was always God, yet who has now become flesh. But when we put ourselves back into the minds of the eager Galileans and Judaeans coming to John for baptism, we realize that they would understand the phrase to mean that Jesus was the Messiah, the true king, who would free Israel from pagan domination.

The next two sections confirm that this is indeed what they had in mind – while constantly hinting to us, as we read their story, that there was much, much more going on. If we are to read John's gospel for all it's worth, we have to learn to hold two strands side by side in our minds, and then, as we get used to that, three or four, or even more. Like someone learning to listen to music, we have to be able to hear the different parts as well as the glorious harmony that they produce when put together. And the music of this gospel is, we may suspect, the sort that makes the angels themselves want to join in.

JOHN 1.35–42

The First Disciples

[35]The following day John was again standing there, with two of his disciples. [36]He saw Jesus walking by, and said, 'Look! There goes God's lamb!'

9

[37]The two disciples heard him say this, and they followed Jesus. [38]Jesus turned and saw them following him.

'What do you want?' he asked.

'Rabbi,' they said (the word means 'teacher'), 'where are you staying?'

[39]'Come and see,' he replied.

So they came, and saw where he was staying, and stayed with him that day. It was late in the afternoon.

[40]One of the two who heard what John said and followed Jesus was Andrew, Simon Peter's brother. [41]The first person he found was his own brother Simon.

'We've found the Messiah!' he said (that means 'the anointed one', like our word 'Christ'). [42]He brought him to Jesus.

Jesus looked at him.

'So,' he said, 'you're Simon, John's son, are you? We'd better call you Cephas!' (That means 'the Rock', like our word 'Peter'.)

I was staying with my uncle in Toronto. I was nineteen at the time. He took me with him for a day on one of his hobbies: clay-pigeon shooting.

I hadn't even seen the sport before, let alone done it. Little disks of clay are propelled from a machine; the shooter stands in various positions, trying to hit the disks as they fly past at different angles and trajectories. I wasn't very good at it, but it was fun and challenging.

The last clay pigeon I had to shoot was coming almost directly at me. It swerved slightly in flight, and all I remember is pulling the trigger and seeing the clay shatter all around me.

My uncle came over to me.

'Good thing you got that one,' he said, 'or it would have got you.'

Up to that moment I hadn't thought of the sport as a two-way affair.

When we read a passage like this we see that there is more of a two-way process going on than the people in the story realized at the time. What Andrew and Simon Peter thought they were doing was looking for the **Messiah**. What they didn't realize was that *the Messiah was looking for them*. Eager in their excitement, they had no idea what this was going to involve.

This is the point, I think, where John, in writing the **gospel**, knows that many readers will begin to identify with characters in the story. It's as well that we pause and ask where that identification might take us. Up to now, the narrative has only told us about **John the Baptist** and the people sent from Jerusalem to check him out. We aren't likely to identify with them. But now here, it seems, are ordinary characters, people on a quest, looking for something. The chances are that you're reading this book because that's been true of you, and perhaps still is. Someone has suggested, as John the Baptist suggested to Andrew and another **disciple**, that you give Jesus a closer look. So here you are.

You approach, polite but a bit cautious. John translates the conversation into your language so you can make it your own. 'Rabbi' means 'teacher'. 'Messiah' means 'anointed one' (the word 'Messiah' is Hebrew or Aramaic, the word 'Christ' is Greek, meaning the same thing). 'Cephas' was the Aramaic word for 'rock' or 'stone', which in Greek is 'Petros', as in our name 'Peter'.

There are four things going on in this quick-fire conversation. Andrew and Simon (and the other, unnamed friend) are looking for the Messiah, and they think they've found him. Jesus is looking for followers, and when he finds them, that gives them a new vocation (Simon becomes 'the Rock', an important but dangerous name). John's readers, out there in the **Gentile** world, would sense Jesus calling and renaming them too. And we, reading this book in the hope of finding out more about Jesus, may discover that he is simultaneously coming to find us. And perhaps to give us new names.

This passage introduces us to a shadowy character who is going to flit across the pages of this gospel several times. There were two disciples of John the Baptist who heard him pointing to Jesus as God's lamb. Only one is named: Andrew, who then finds Simon Peter his brother. Who was the other one? All sorts of answers have been given, and none of them is without difficulty. But the simplest answer is that this was one of the other early disciples who met and followed Jesus right from the start. Since he isn't named, here or elsewhere, it is not impossible that we are here meeting the author of the book, or at least the one who told the stories on which the book was based.

We shall say more about this later. But there is quite a good chance that this was John, the brother of James, one of Zebedee's sons. A young man at the time – quite likely still in his teens – he remembered those early days, and the conversations with Jesus, with all the vivid recollection that goes with a life-changing moment. That's why, though he translates the key words so his readers will understand, he doesn't want to change the actual words he remembers so well. You don't alter the foundation of the house you're living in. When you go looking for Jesus, and discover that he's looking for you, you will remember that day for ever.

JOHN 1.43-51

Philip and Nathanael

⁴³The next day Jesus decided to go to Galilee, where he found Philip. 'Follow me,' he said to him.

11

⁴⁴Philip came from Bethsaida, the town where Andrew and Peter hailed from. ⁴⁵Philip found Nathanael.

'We've found him!' he said. 'The one Moses wrote about in the law! And the prophets, too! We've found him! It's Jesus, Joseph's son, from Nazareth!'

⁴⁶'Really?' replied Nathanael. 'Are you telling me that something good can come out of Nazareth?'

'Come and see,' replied Philip.

⁴⁷Jesus saw Nathanael coming towards him.

'Here he comes,' he said. 'Look at him! He's a real Israelite. Genuine through and through.'

⁴⁸'How did you get to know me?' asked Nathanael.

'Oh,' replied Jesus, 'I saw you under the fig tree, before Philip spoke to you.'

⁴⁹'Rabbi,' replied Nathanael, 'you're the son of God! You're the king of Israel!'

⁵⁰'Wait a minute,' said Jesus. 'Are you telling me that you believe just because I told you I saw you under the fig tree? You'll see a lot more than that!

⁵¹'In fact,' he went on, 'I'm telling you the solemn truth. You'll see heaven opened, and God's angels going up and down upon the son of man.'

Jacob was a schemer and twister. All his early life he had one eye on the main chance, especially if it meant getting one up on his older twin, Esau. In fact, even the story of how they were born included the telling detail: he'd been holding on to his brother's heel. Trying to trip him up, even in the womb. And the habit stuck. He tricked Esau out of his birthright, and out of his father's blessing. Eventually the tables turned, and Esau tried to kill him. It was time for Jacob to leave in a hurry. You can read the story, fresh and vivid from millennia ago, in Genesis 25–28.

When Jacob was running away, with not a penny to his name and nothing but the clothes on his back, he had a dream. He saw a ladder with its foot on the ground and its top reaching to **heaven**. God's angels were going up and down on it. The Lord himself stood beside him, and promised him that he would bring him back to his land in peace and prosperity.

It is this passage that Jesus seems to be referring to when he says to Nathanael that he and the other **disciples** (the 'you' in verse 51 is plural) will see heaven opened, with the angels of God going up and down upon – the **son of man**. This is a very strange picture, and to begin with it's hard to see what Nathanael and the others might have made of it, what John thinks we should make of it, and indeed what Jesus might have meant by it. Since it's obviously important within the **gospel**, concluding the first chapter, in which so many of the gospel's great themes have been introduced, we'd better look at it a bit more closely.

The point about Jacob's ladder was that it showed that God was there with him, in that place. Jacob called the place 'Bethel', that is, 'God's house'. After he had come back to the land, and when, much later, his descendants had been established in possession of it, Bethel became one of the great sanctuaries of Israel, one of the places where early Israelite worship was carried on. The tradition of Jacob's dream, of the angels going up and down on the ladder, would then be connected with the belief that when you worshipped God in his house, God was really present, with his angels coming and going to link heaven and earth.

This is probably the clue we're looking for. A great deal of John's gospel has to do with the way in which Jesus fulfils the promises made concerning the **Temple** – and also goes beyond them, pioneering the new way in which the living God will be present with his people. This was hinted at in the Prologue (1.14). When John says that the **Word** became flesh 'and lived among us', the word for 'lived' is a word associated with the presence of God 'tabernacling' or 'pitching his tent' in our midst. The thought of a tent in which God lived would send Jewish minds back to the tabernacle in the wilderness at the time of the **Exodus**, and from there to the Temple in Jerusalem where God's presence was promised.

Verse 51, then, seems to be a tight-packed and evocative way of saying: 'Don't think that all you will see is one or two remarkable acts of insight, such as you witnessed when I showed you that I knew about you before you even appeared. What you'll see from now on is the reality towards which Jacob's ladder, and even the Temple itself, was pointing like a signpost. If you follow me, you'll be watching what it looks like when heaven and earth are open to each other. You won't necessarily see the angels themselves, but you'll see things happening which show that they're there all right.'

The earlier part of the passage is meant, I think, to be funny, almost as comic light relief before the solemn and serious promise at the end. Nathanael, who comes from Cana (John tells us this in 21.2), can't believe that anything good would come out of the rival village, Nazareth, a short distance up the hill. A cryptic word from Jesus, and suddenly he not only believes it's possible, he gives Jesus the exalted title of **son of God**! Jesus seems as surprised, and amused, as we are in reading it.

We should, I think, continue to understand 'son of God' here as a messianic title, explained by 'king of Israel' which immediately follows it. John, as we know, means more than this, but I don't think

13

Nathanael yet does. Indeed, that's part of the point of the closing remark. Jesus may be 'the son of man'; though in what sense he, or John, intend that phrase remains for the moment uncertain. What matters is that something much greater than a mere **Messiah** is here. When you're with Jesus, it is as though you're in the house of God, the Temple itself, with God's angels coming and going, and God's own presence there beside you.

That promise, of course, remains as true today as it was then. That, as John explains much later (20.31), is why he's writing this book.

JOHN 2.1–12

Water into Wine

[1]On the third day there was a wedding at Cana in Galilee. Jesus' mother was there, [2]and Jesus and his disciples were also invited to the wedding.

[3]The wine ran out.

Jesus' mother came over to him.

'They haven't got any wine!' she said.

[4]'Oh, Mother,' replied Jesus, 'What's that got to do with you and me? My time hasn't come yet.'

[5]His mother spoke to the servants.

'Do whatever he tells you,' she said.

[6]Six stone water-jars were standing there, ready for use in the Jewish purification rites. Each held about twenty or thirty gallons.

[7]'Fill the jars with water,' said Jesus to the servants. And they filled them, right up to the brim.

[8]'Now draw some out', he said, 'and take it to the chief steward.' They did so.

[9]When the chief steward tasted the water that had turned into wine (he didn't know where it had come from, but the servants who had drawn the water knew), he called the bridegroom.

[10]'What everybody normally does', he said, 'is to serve the good wine first, and then the worse stuff when people have had plenty to drink. But you've kept the good wine till now!'

[11]This event, in Cana of Galilee, was the first of Jesus' signs. He displayed his glory, and his disciples believed in him.

[12]After this, he went down to Capernaum, with his mother, his brothers and his disciples. He remained there for a few days.

One of the first events I ever organized was a treasure hunt. It was during the school holidays, when I was about ten or eleven. I invited all my friends from neighbouring houses and streets to come and join in.

With my mother's careful help, I planned each of the clues in cryptic rhyming couplets, and worked out the different things people would find as they followed them. I remember feeling nervous as fifteen or twenty children poured out of the house, eager to follow up the clues they had been given. Would they understand them all right? Would they get bored and give up? Would some be much better at it than others? I needn't have worried. The event was a success, and everyone had fun.

John's **gospel** is planned as a kind of treasure hunt, with careful and sometimes cryptic clues laid for us to follow. Now that he's set the scene with the opening stories about **John the Baptist** and Jesus' early followers, he gives us the first clue, telling us that it's the first one so we know where we are. He will tell us about the second one, too, two chapters later; from then on, we're on our own, and he wants us to use our initiative and imagination in following the clues to the very end. I won't spoil it for you by telling you the answer at the moment, but if you wanted to sit down and read right through the gospel you might be able to work it out for yourself.

The word he uses for 'clue' is 'sign' (verse 11). He is setting up a series of signposts to take us through his story. The signs are all occasions when Jesus did, you might say, what he'd just promised Nathanael that he would do. They are moments when, to people who watch with at least a little **faith**, the angels of God are going up and coming down at the place where Jesus is. They are moments when **heaven** is opened, when the transforming power of God's love bursts in to the present world.

That's why it simply won't do, despite what some people have said, to see the things that Jesus did, and the stories about them in this gospel and the other ones, as pleasant but imaginary legends – things that didn't actually happen but which 'illustrate' some supposedly deeper, more 'spiritual' truth. The whole point of the 'signs' is that they are moments when heaven and earth intersect with each other. (That's what the Jews believed happened in the **Temple**.) The point is not that they are stories which couldn't have happened in real life, but which point away from earth to a heavenly reality.

Whatever people today may think actually happened – and the more you get to know about Jesus the more you realize that this sort of thing was precisely what you should expect with him around – we should be in no doubt that what John badly wants to tell us is that with these events the life of heaven came down to earth. That's why one of the motto texts for the whole gospel is 'the **Word** became flesh' (1.14).

The present story has all the elements that we shall come to know well as we work through the gospel. It is about transformation: the different dimension of reality that comes into being when Jesus is present and when, as Mary tells the servants, people do whatever Jesus tells them.

This is one of only two occasions we meet Jesus' mother in this gospel, the other being at the foot of the cross (chapter 19). This is important, because Jesus' strange remark in verse 4, 'My time hasn't come yet', looks on, through many other references to his 'time', until at last the time does come, and the glory is revealed fully, as he dies on the cross. That event, for John, is the ultimate moment when heaven and earth meet. That is when it takes all the faith in the world to see the glory hidden in the shame: the creative Word present as a weak, dying human being.

But events like this one point on to that moment. The wedding is a foretaste of the great heavenly feast in store for God's people (see Revelation 21.2). The water-jars, used for Jewish purification rites, are a sign that God is doing a new thing from within the old Jewish system, bringing purification to Israel and the world in a whole new way.

The wedding itself, in the town where Nathanael came from, would probably involve almost the whole village, and several people from neighbouring ones too; which is why Mary, her son and his friends were invited. Running out of wine was not just inconvenient, but a social disaster and disgrace. The family would have to live with the shame of it for a long time to come; bride and groom might regard it as bringing bad luck on their married life. Though Jesus hereafter addresses himself to other kinds of problems, we are already witnessing the strange compassion which comes where people are in need and deals with that need in unexpected ways.

The transformation from water to wine is of course meant by John to signify the effect that Jesus can have, can still have today, on people's lives. He came, as he says later, that we might have **life** in all its fullness (10.10). You might want to pray through this story with your own failures and disappointments in mind – remembering that transformation only came when someone took Mary's words seriously: 'Do whatever he tells you.'

One final point. What do you think John is hinting at when he says that all this took place 'on the third day'?

JOHN 2.13–25

Jesus in the Temple

¹³It was nearly time for the Judaean Passover, and Jesus went up to Jerusalem.

¹⁴In the Temple he found people selling cows, sheep and doves, and the money-changers sitting there. ¹⁵He made a whip out of cords and drove them all out of the Temple, sheep, cows and all. He spilt the money-changers' coins onto the ground, and knocked over their tables.

[16]'Take these things away!' he said to the people selling doves. 'You mustn't turn my father's house into a market!'

[17]His disciples remembered that it was written, 'The zeal of your house has eaten me up.'

[18]The Judaeans had this response for him.'What sign are you going to show us', they said, 'to explain why you're doing this?'

[19]'Destroy this Temple,' replied Jesus, 'and I'll raise it up in three days.'

[20]'It's taken forty-six years to build this Temple,' responded the Judaeans, 'and are you going to raise it up in three days?' [21]But he was speaking about the 'temple' of his body. [22]So when he was raised from the dead, his disciples remembered that he had said this, and they believed the Bible and the word which Jesus had spoken.

[23]While he was in Jerusalem during the Passover festival, several people came to trust in his name, because they had seen the signs he did. [24]But Jesus didn't entrust himself to them. He knew everything, [25]and had no need for anyone to give him information about people. He himself knew what was inside people.

Imagine the scene in a school. The pupils are all taking their end-of-year exams. The teachers are preparing for a big Open Day when parents and friends will come to visit. Everyone is excited. It's the biggest moment in the school year.

Suddenly the door of the head teacher's office bursts open. In walks a pupil, with a few friends behind him. He goes straight to the desk where the secretary is organizing a pile of examination scripts, and turns the desk upside down, scattering the scripts all over the room. He proceeds into the head teacher's private room, where with a single sweep of his arm he knocks to the floor all the letters and papers, the invitations and arrangements, so carefully made for the big day that's coming up.

He turns on the astonished onlookers. 'This whole place is a disgrace!' he shouts. 'It's corrupt from top to bottom! You ought to be ashamed of yourselves!'

Before he can get away, the head teacher himself arrives. 'What right have you got to behave like this?' he asks.

'You can fail me if you like,' replies the pupil. 'You can throw me out. But I shall go to the university. I'm going to train as a lawyer. And one day I'll put an end to corruption like this. Your system is finished!' Then, before they can stop him, he leaves.

Now all such stories are only partly parallel to the astonishing scene in the **Temple**. No illustration can do justice to what Jesus did; we have to understand the event itself, unique as it was, and to understand as

17

well what John wants us to see within it. This, too, is a moment of angels going to and fro between **heaven** and earth.

The Temple was the beating heart of Judaism. It wasn't just, as it were, a church on a street corner. It was the centre of worship and music, of politics and society, of national celebration and mourning. It was also the place where you would find more animals (alive and dead) than anywhere else. But, towering above all these, it was of course the place where Israel's God, YHWH, had promised to live in the midst of his people. It was the focal point of the nation, and of the national way of life.

And this was where the then unknown prophet from Galilee came in and turned everything upside down. People used to the Bible story can forget how shocking it must have been – which is why it's good to find modern illustrations of similar, though hardly identical, scenes. And the questions it all raises are: what was wrong with the Temple? Why did Jesus do what he did? And what does his answer mean, when they asked him for a sign?

Before even that, there's another question to be considered. People who know the other **gospels** in the New Testament will realize that they contain a very similar incident. But in Matthew, Mark and Luke it occurs at the end of Jesus' public career, when he arrives in Jerusalem for the last time, rather than at the beginning as it does here. All sorts of theories exist as to which is right – or whether, even, Jesus did something like this twice.

In favour of putting the incident at the beginning, as John does, is the fact that Matthew, Mark and Luke don't have Jesus in Jerusalem at all during his adult life, so the final journey is the only place where it can happen. John, however, has Jesus going to and fro to Jerusalem a good deal throughout his short career. And if he had done something like this at the beginning, it would explain certain things very well: why, for instance, people came from Jerusalem to Galilee to check him out (e.g. Mark 3.22; 7.1), and why, when the **high priest** finally decided it was time to act, they already felt they had a case against him (John 11.47–53).

But there is no doubt what John thinks it all means. It is Passover time; he has already told us that Jesus is God's Passover lamb, and now he goes to Jerusalem at the time when liberation, freedom, rescue from slavery was being celebrated. Somehow, John wants us to understand, what Jesus did in the Temple is a hint at the new meaning he is giving to Passover. This will be important for the other Passover moments in the story: in chapter 6, for instance, and of course in the final scenes which begin in chapter 12.

It's also a hint – and a strong one – as to what Jesus thinks of the Temple itself. Clearly, he regards it as corrupt, and under God's judgment.

The trade, the marketplace atmosphere, isn't what it was supposed to be there for.

But the meaning that begins to grow here, like a seed putting out the first shoots that show what sort of a shrub it's going to be, has to do with Jesus' own fate. When they ask what he thinks he's up to, and request some kind of sign to show them what it all means, he speaks, very cryptically, about his own death and **resurrection**.

He is the true temple: he is the **Word** made flesh, the place where the glory of God has chosen to make his dwelling. The Jews had ancient traditions about the Temple being destroyed and rebuilt. It had happened before, and some thought it would happen again. Herod the Great had begun a programme of rebuilding the Temple, and now, forty-six years later, one of his sons was completing it. Jesus takes the traditions and applies them to himself. He is the reality to which the Temple itself points. His death and resurrection will be the reality to which the whole Passover celebration points.

In the two vivid scenes of chapter 2, John has introduced us to almost all the major themes of the gospel story, and has given us food for thought about where it's all going. But, as so often, he ends with a hint as to how people should respond. If you see the signs Jesus is doing, then trust him. Believe in him. Jesus, after all, is the one who knows you through and through.

JOHN 3.1–13

Jesus and Nicodemus

¹There was a man of the Pharisees called Nicodemus, a ruler of the Judaeans. ²He came to Jesus by night.

'Rabbi,' he said to him. 'We know that you're a teacher who's come from God. Nobody can do these signs that you're doing, unless God is with him.'

³'Let me tell you the solemn truth,' replied Jesus. 'Unless someone has been born from above, they won't be able to see God's kingdom.'

⁴'How can someone possibly be born,' asked Nicodemus, 'when they're old? You're not telling me they can go back a second time into the mother's womb and be born, are you?'

⁵'I'm telling you the solemn truth,' replied Jesus. 'Unless someone is born from water and spirit, they can't enter God's kingdom. ⁶Flesh is born from flesh, but spirit is born from spirit. ⁷Don't be surprised that I said to you, You must be born from above. ⁸The wind blows where it wants to, and you hear the sound it makes; but you don't know where it's coming from or where it's going to. That's what it's like with someone who is born from the spirit.'

⁹'How can this be so?' asked Nicodemus.

¹⁰'Well, well!' replied Jesus. 'You're a teacher of Israel, and yet you don't know about all this? ¹¹I'm telling you the solemn truth: we're talking about things we know about. We're giving evidence about things we've seen. But you won't admit our evidence. ¹²If I told you earthly things and you don't believe, how will it be if I tell you heavenly things? Are you going to believe then? ¹³And nobody has gone up into heaven except the one who came down from heaven, the son of man.'

I have lost my birth certificate.

It's the sort of thing that happens when you move house, which we did not long ago. I know where it was in the old house. It may have been accidentally thrown away; but I suspect it was put into a very, very safe place, and the place was so safe that I still haven't found it.

Fortunately, I don't need it at the moment. I have a passport and other documents. Sooner or later, if it doesn't show up, I shall have to get a replacement, which means going back to the town where I was born and paying to have a new copy made from the register there.

But, of course, the one thing that a birth certificate isn't needed for is to prove that a birth took place. Here I am, a human being; obviously I must have been born. The fact that at the moment I can't officially prove when and where is a minor detail.

When Christians discuss the 'new birth', the 'second birth' or the 'birth from above', they often forget this. Some people experience their entry into Christian **faith** as a huge, tumultuous event, with a dramatic build-up, a painful moment of decision and then tidal waves of relief, joy, exhilaration, forgiveness and love. They are then easily tempted – and there are movements of thought within Western culture which make this temptation all the more powerful – to think that this moment itself is the centre of what it means to be a Christian, as though what God wanted was simply to give people a single wonderful spiritual experience, to be remembered ever afterwards with a warm glow.

But that's a bit like someone framing their birth certificate, hanging it on the wall, and insisting on showing it to everyone who comes into the house. What matters for most purposes is not that once upon a time you were born – though of course sometimes it matters that you can prove when and where you were born. What matters is that you are alive *now*, and that your present life, day by day and moment by moment, is showing evidence of health and strength and purpose. Physical birth is often painful and difficult, for the baby as well as for the mother. But you don't spend your life talking about what a difficult birth you had, unless for some tragic reason it has left you with medical problems. You get on with being the person you now are.

So when Jesus talks to Nicodemus about the new birth, and when John highlights this conversation by making it the first of several in-depth discussions Jesus has in this **gospel**, we shouldn't suppose that this means that we should spend all our time thinking about the moment of our own spiritual birth. It matters that it happened, of course. Sadly, there are many, inside the church as well as outside, whose present state suggests that one ought to go back to examine whether in fact a real spiritual birth took place at all. But where there are signs of **life** it's more important to feed and nurture it than to spend much time going over and over what happened at the moment of birth.

In fact, what Jesus says here to Nicodemus is more sharply focused than we sometimes imagine. The Judaism that Nicodemus and Jesus both knew had a good deal to do with *being born into the right family*. What mattered was being a child of Abraham. Of course, other things mattered too, but this was basic. Now, Jesus is saying, God is starting a new family in which this ordinary birth isn't enough. You need to be born all over again, born 'from above'. (The same word, here, can mean 'a second time' and 'from above'. We should probably understand both, with the emphasis on 'from above'; the point, as with 1.12–13, is that the initiative remains God's.)

The new birth Jesus is talking about is the same thing that has been spoken of in 1.33. 'Water and **spirit**' here must mean the double **baptism**: baptism in water, which brings people into the **kingdom**-movement begun by **John the Baptist** and continued by Jesus' **disciples** (3.22; 4.1–2), and baptism in the spirit, the new life, bubbling up from within, that Jesus offers, which is the main thing that this whole book is about.

The two are closely joined. Nobody in the early church supposed that spirit-baptism mattered so much that you could do without water-baptism. From time to time the problem arose of people assuming that as long as you had water-baptism you didn't need to worry about the new spiritual life (see, for instance, 1 Corinthians 10.1–13). But the point in this passage is that this double-sided new birth, which brings you into the visible community of Jesus' followers (water-baptism) and gives you the new life of the spirit welling up like a spring of water inside you (spirit-baptism), was now required for membership in God's kingdom. Indeed (as Jesus says in verse 3), without it you can't even *see* God's kingdom. You can't glimpse it, let alone get into it.

As with 1.12–13, the point of this is that God's kingdom is now thrown open to anyone and everyone. The spirit is on the move, like a fresh spring breeze (verse 8; part of the point here is that the word for 'wind', in both Hebrew and Greek, is the same word as you'd use for 'spirit'), and no human family, tribe, organization or system can keep up with it. Opening the window and letting the breeze in can be very inconvenient, especially for the Nicodemuses of this world who suppose they have got things tidied up, labelled and sorted into neat piles.

But unless we are prepared to listen to this dangerous message we aren't ready to listen to the gospel at all. In verses 10–13 we have the first of many passages in which Jesus speaks about a new knowledge – indeed, a new sort of knowing. It's a way of knowing that comes from God, from **heaven**.

It's humbling for Nicodemus to have to be told this. He is, after all, a respected and senior teacher. But this way of knowing, and the new knowledge we get through it, is given by the mysterious '**son of man**'. As we were told in 1.51, he is now the ladder which joins the two dimensions of God's world, the heavenly and the earthly. If we want to understand not only the heavenly world, but the way in which God is now joining heaven and earth together, we must listen to him, and walk with him on the road he is now to take.

JOHN 3.14–21

The Snake and the Love of God

[14]'So, just as Moses lifted up the snake in the desert, in the same way the son of man must be lifted up, [15]so that everyone who believes in him may share in the life of God's new age. [16]This, you see, is how much God loved the world: enough to give his only, special son, so that everyone who believes in him should not be lost but should share in the life of God's new age. [17]After all, God didn't send the son into the world to condemn the world, but so that the world could be saved by him.

[18]'Anyone who believes in him is not condemned. But anyone who doesn't believe is condemned already, because they didn't believe in the name of God's only, special son. [19]And this is the condemnation: that light has come into the world, and people loved darkness rather than light, because what they were doing was evil. [20]For everyone who does evil hates the light; people like that don't come to the light, in case their deeds get shown up and reproved. [21]But people who do the truth come to the light, so that it can become clear that what they have done has been done in God.'

'And mind you watch out for snakes!'

My wife gave me a final warning before I set off into the hills. The footpaths had been closed for several months because of a widespread and infectious animal disease. Many creatures that normally kept away from regular footpaths had, apparently, spent the spring enjoying a new-found freedom. We don't have many dangerous snakes in the British Isles, but the viper is dangerous enough. And, to be honest, I didn't know exactly what I would do if I met one.

Fortunately, I didn't see one on the walk. But it sent my mind back to the way in which the symbol of the snake has been used in many cultures over many thousands of years. From the snake in the garden of Eden to the serpent Ananta in some branches of Hinduism, to the mythic serpent-ancestor of the Aztecs and the 'old god of nature' in parts of Africa to this day; from poetry to art and medicine, not least psychoanalysis; the figure of the serpent or snake has haunted human imagination from time immemorial.

In many cultures, the serpent is seen as positive and powerful, though dangerous. In many others, not least in some parts of the Jewish and Christian traditions, the serpent is seen as a strong negative force, symbolizing the evil in the world and in all of us. The question of what to do about the serpent is a way of asking the question of what to do about evil – or what different cultures have designated as evil.

The present passage gives a clear and confident answer, which has itself been powerful in subsequent thought and culture. Verse 14 looks back to the incident described in Numbers 21.5–8. During their wandering in the wilderness, the Israelites grumbled against Moses, and were punished by poisonous snakes invading the camp, killing many of them. God gave Moses the remedy: he was to make a serpent out of bronze, put it on a pole and hold it up for people to look at. Anyone who looked at the serpent on the pole would live. The serpent entwined around the pole, a symbol which appears in other cultures too, remains to this day as a sign of healing, used by various medical organizations.

The bronze serpent was thereafter stored in the Tabernacle as a sacred object, until, much later, King Hezekiah discovered that the people were worshipping it, and broke it to pieces (2 Kings 18.4). In the time of Jesus, one Jewish writer found it necessary to emphasize that it wasn't the bronze serpent itself that had saved the Israelites, but the saving power of God (Wisdom of Solomon 16.7). All this shows the strange power of the symbol, and highlights even more the importance of verse 14 for understanding what Jesus had come to do.

This, in fact, is the only place in the New Testament where the bronze serpent is referred to. Here it points clearly to the death of Jesus. Moses put the serpent on a pole, and lifted it up so the people could see it; even so, the **son of man** must be lifted up, so that everyone who believes in him may have **the life of God's coming age**. Humankind as a whole has been smitten with a deadly disease. The only cure is to look at the son of man dying on the cross, and find **life** through believing in him.

This is very deep and mysterious, but we must ask: how can the crucifixion of Jesus be like putting the snake on a pole? Wasn't the snake the problem, not the solution? Surely John isn't suggesting that Jesus was like the poisonous snakes that had been attacking the people?

No, he isn't. What he is saying, and will continue to say in several ways right up to his account of the crucifixion, is that the evil which was and is in the world, deep-rooted within us all, was somehow allowed to take out its full force on Jesus. When we look at him hanging on the cross (or 'lifted up', as John says here and several times later in the **gospel**; the cross is an 'elevation', almost a 'glorification'), what we are looking at is the result of the evil in which we are all stuck. And we are seeing what God has done about it.

We are seeing, in particular, what God's own love looks like. John refers us back to 1.18, and behind that to 1.1–2, in order to say: when Jesus died on the cross, that was the full and dramatic display of God's own love. It wasn't a messy accident; it wasn't God letting the worst happen to someone else. The cross is at the heart of John's amazing new picture of who God is. He is now to be known as the God who is both father and son, and the son is revealed, 'lifted up', when he dies under the weight of the world's evil. The cross is the ultimate ladder set up between **heaven** and earth.

But evil isn't then healed, as it were, automatically. Precisely because evil lurks deep within each of us, for healing to take place we must ourselves be involved in the process. This doesn't mean that we just have to try a lot harder to be good. You might as well try to teach a snake to sing. All we can do, just as it was all the Israelites could do, is to look and trust: to look at Jesus, to see in him the full display of God's saving love, and to trust in him.

Here there opens up the great divide, which John describes in terms of darkness and light (see 1.4–5). Believing in Jesus means coming to the light, the light of God's new creation. Not believing means remaining in the darkness. The darkness (and those who embrace it) must be condemned, not because it offends against some arbitrary laws which God made up for the fun of it, and certainly not because it has to do with the material, created world rather than with a supposed 'spiritual' world. It must be condemned because evil is destroying and defacing the present world, and preventing people coming forward into God's new world (that is, **the life of God's coming age**).

But the point of the whole story is that you don't have to be condemned. You don't have to let the snake kill you. God's action in the crucifixion of Jesus has planted a sign in the middle of history. And the sign says: believe, and live.

JOHN 3.22–36

The Bridegroom and His Friend

[22]After this, Jesus and his disciples went into the countryside of Judaea, and he stayed there with them and baptized. [23]John, too, was baptizing at Aenon, close to Salim. There was plenty of water there, and people came to him and were baptized. [24]This, of course, was before John had been put into prison.

[25]There was, perhaps inevitably, a dispute between the disciples of John and a Judaean, on the subject of purification. [26]They came to John.

'Rabbi,' they said. 'Remember the man who was with you beyond the Jordan, the one you gave evidence about? Well, look! He's baptizing, and everyone's going to him!'

[27]'Nobody can receive anything unless heaven first gives it,' replied John. [28]'You yourselves can bear me out that I said I wasn't the Messiah, but that I was sent ahead of him. [29]It's the bridegroom who gets the bride. The bridegroom's friend, who stands nearby and hears him, is very happy when he hears the bridegroom's voice. So, you see, my joy is now complete. [30]He must increase, but I must decrease.'

[31]The one who comes from above is over everything. The one who is from the earth has an earthly character, and what he says has 'earth' written all over it. The one who comes from heaven is above all. [32]He gives evidence about what he has heard and seen, and nobody accepts his evidence. [33]The one who does accept his evidence has put his signature to the fact that God is true. [34]The one God sent, you see, speaks God's words, because he gives the spirit lavishly. [35]The father loves the son and has given everything into his hand. [36]Anyone who believes in the son shares in the life of God's new age. Anyone who doesn't believe in the son won't see life, but God's wrath rests on him.

Millions of television viewers around the world remember the moment when Lady Diana Spencer got the words wrong in her marriage to Prince Charles. It wasn't a serious mistake – her husband had rather a lot of names, and she got two of them in the wrong order – but I suspect that clergy who were watching will have smiled at several other similar memories.

Whenever I take a wedding in church I know that all the key people are nervous. Some parents, of course, have already seen several children get married, and one more wedding is not a big strain. But for most it is a defining moment in their whole lives. As for the bride and groom, and the attendants who are with them on either side, this is like suddenly acting in a strange and wonderful play in front of all their family and friends. No wonder several of them say things, and sometimes do things, in the wrong order.

But there is another tension which can creep in, as well as stage fright. Sometimes one set of parents disapproves of the match. Sometimes old friends of either the bride or groom are anxious about it. And sometimes there is someone there who has long wished that they could be marrying this person instead. They may be putting a brave face on it, but underneath they are grieving.

That's the image that **John the Baptist** draws on when he speaks cheerfully to his followers about the success that Jesus and his **disciples** seem to be having in baptizing people. John's followers seem to be assuming that he will be jealous. Nobody knew at that stage, of course, that John would shortly be put in prison by Herod, and would lose his life not long after that. His followers must have expected his movement to go on and on, and they were disturbed that someone who had been part of it was now setting up an independent effort. John's response is not only that it doesn't matter, but that it has to be this way. Jesus is the one who is carrying forward God's purposes. He himself has done what he had to do. He is like the bridegroom's friend, the 'best man' as some cultures call it. He has no intention of trying to steal the bride at the last minute.

The picture of the bridegroom with his bride is not just a convenient illustration, showing that John's followers are jealous of Jesus and that John is refusing to see things in those terms. In the Old Testament and some Jewish traditions, the coming **Messiah** was seen as the bridegroom par excellence, the one who would come and make Israel his bride. Behind this again, of course, is the equally important tradition that YHWH, Israel's God, would betroth Israel to himself as his bride. Whether or not the Baptist thought of this at the time – his mind seems to be focused on the fact that Jesus is Israel's Messiah, the coming king, and that he himself is not – the writer certainly intends us to think of it.

John the evangelist also intends us to see, not for the last time in the **gospel**, the way in which different characters in the story of Jesus have to learn, as C. S. Lewis once put it, to play great parts without pride and small parts without shame. At the very end of the gospel (21.20–23), Peter is reminded that what counts is not comparing yourself with other people and seeing whether your status is higher or lower than theirs, but simply following Jesus. Here, already, John the Baptist adds to the evidence he's given about Jesus' messiahship, by insisting that if Jesus is prospering, and people are going to him, that means that he, who had pointed to him, should celebrate rather than be miserable or jealous.

The last paragraph of the section has sometimes been seen as the continuation of what John the Baptist said to his followers, but it's much more likely to be the writer's comment on the whole chapter so far. (The same problem occurs at several points in this book, where a long speech seems to merge effortlessly into the writer's comment. In fact, the second section of the chapter (3.14–21) has sometimes been seen, as a whole or in part, as the continuation of Jesus' speech which began in verse 5.) When we meet a passage like this, we should take it slowly and prayerfully; it is the writer's way of saying 'So: where are *you* in this picture?'

He is contrasting 'the one from above' – Jesus, in other words – with 'the one from the earth'. This doesn't mean John the Baptist; he, after all, was 'sent from God' (1.6; 1.33; 3.27). There are plenty of people whose life and teaching are 'from the earth', and a good many of them were competing with Jesus and John, and with the early church, for the ears, minds and hearts of both Jews and **Gentiles**. So too, today: who do people trust? Who do they listen to and follow?

All too often, alas, they trust those whose message has no breath of **heaven** about it, no sign of **life** from the hidden dimension of God's world. Meanwhile, as we saw already in 1.10–11, most of those to whom Jesus was sent did not, and do not, receive what he says. The end of that road is wrath, not because God is a tyrant or a bully but because earth, and all that is earthbound, will corrupt and decay. But anyone who does receive his **word** – who accepts that God has spoken truly in him, is giving the **spirit** through him, is pouring out his love through him into the world – such a person already has within himself or herself the life that, like the son, comes from heaven.

JOHN 4.1–15

The Woman of Samaria

¹So when Jesus knew that the Pharisees had heard that he was making more disciples than John, and was baptizing them ²(Jesus himself didn't baptize people; it was his disciples who were doing it), ³he left Judaea and went back to Galilee.

⁴He had to go through Samaria, ⁵and he came to a town in Samaria named Sychar. It was near the place which Jacob gave to his son Joseph. ⁶Jacob's well was there. So Jesus, tired from the journey, sat down there by the well. It was about midday.

⁷A Samaritan woman came to draw water, and Jesus spoke to her.

'Give me a drink,' he said. ⁸(The disciples had gone off into the town to buy food.)

⁹'What!' said the Samaritan woman. 'You, a Jew, asking for a drink from me, a woman, and a Samaritan at that?' (Jews, you see, don't have any dealings with Samaritans.)

¹⁰'If only you'd known God's gift', replied Jesus, 'and who it is that's saying to you, "Give me a drink", you'd have asked him, and he would have given you living water.'

¹¹'But sir,' replied the woman, 'you haven't got a bucket! And the well's deep! So how were you thinking of getting living water? ¹²Are you greater than our father Jacob, who gave us the well, and drank of it himself, with his sons and his animals?'

¹³'Everyone who drinks this water', Jesus replied, 'will get thirsty again. ¹⁴But anyone who drinks the water I'll give them won't ever be thirsty again. No: the water I'll give them will become a spring of water welling up to the life of God's new age.'

¹⁵'Sir,' the woman said, 'give me this water! Then I won't be thirsty any more, and I won't have to come here to draw from the well.'

'Have you heard about Simon?' a friend asked me. 'He's become a Samaritan!'

I knew what he meant. I did not think for a minute that our mutual friend had gone off to the Middle East to join the tiny sect who still live in the middle of ancient Samaria, keeping alive a way of life that goes back to long before the time of Jesus. To visit the Samaritans, particularly to watch their Passover celebration, as many tourists do, offers a fascinating glimpse into the time and world of the Bible. But that wasn't what my friend meant.

Today, the 'Samaritans' have become world-famous as an organization for helping people in extreme distress. They listen, on the telephone or in person, to the horrible things that have happened to their fellow human beings, and try to talk calmly through the problems and help the sufferer accept the way things are and see the way forward. Many thousands of people have been restrained from suicide, or other extreme acts, through this usually unseen ministry.

The organization, ironically, is named after the people whom the first-century Jews regarded as the worst kind of outcasts. In Luke's **gospel**, Jesus told a story about a Samaritan who had gone to the aid of a Jew in desperate need when his own people had ignored him (Luke 10.30–37). That's where the name comes from. But here in John's gospel, too, the Samaritans are important, and this is the passage that makes them so.

Samaria is the name given to the land in between Galilee to the north and Judaea to the south. If Jesus and his followers were travelling from the one to the other, through Samaria was the natural route. Natural, that is, geographically; but sometimes the Samaritans would attack pilgrims going from Galilee to Jerusalem, and so many would go a different way, down the Jordan valley to Jericho and then up the hill from there to Jerusalem. That, in fact, is what Jesus and his followers did on their last journey together.

But this time they went north through Samaria, apparently without trouble. And there, in the heat of the day, Jesus found himself alone by Jacob's Well (which is still there), when along came a woman.

Newspapers and magazines sometimes run a feature entitled 'What is Wrong with this Picture?' They don't mean that it's a bad photograph. They mean that someone in the picture is doing something so unusual as to seem crazy – trying to fix a computer with a sledgehammer, or sitting down to a meal consisting of daffodils and tulips. Now, the picture we see in the present passage has several things, in that sense, 'wrong' with it, and they all matter. They may not look odd to us, but we only understand the passage when we see how it would have looked to anyone at the time it was written.

For a start, Jesus was known already as a holy man, leading a movement to bring Israel back to God. (John's readers know that he is more than that, but we must learn to think with the minds of his followers at the time.) In that culture, many devout Jewish men would not have allowed themselves to be alone with a woman. If it was unavoidable that they should be, they would certainly not have entered into conversation with her. The risk, they would have thought, was too high – risk of impurity, risk of gossip, risk ultimately of being drawn into immorality. And yet Jesus is talking to this woman. Later in the chapter John shows how startled the **disciples** were by this (4.27).

Second, the woman is of course a Samaritan. Ever since some of the Jewish **exiles** had come back from Babylon, to find that the central section of their ancient territory was occupied by a group who claimed to be the true descendants of Abraham, and who opposed their return, there had been constant trouble. Sometimes it had broken out into actual skirmishes, with bloodshed and murder. But mostly it was simply a matter of not mixing. The Jews wouldn't have anything to do with the Samaritans. They would, especially, not share eating and drinking vessels with them. And yet Jesus is asking this woman for a drink.

Third, compounding both of these problems, the woman is obviously a bad character. The normal time for women to visit the well, set as it was at some distance from the town, would be at a cooler time of day, most likely first thing in the morning or late in the afternoon. This woman has come at the time when she is least likely to meet anyone – at least, anyone who knows her, her past and her immoral lifestyle. The last thing she would want would be to rub shoulders with the other women of the town, and they would feel the same about her. Jesus will presently show that he knows all about this. And yet he engages her in conversation – conversation with a teasing, double-meaning flavour to it.

The multiple meanings are, as we shall see, typical of the kind of conversation John reports. Again and again in this gospel Jesus talks to people who misunderstand what he says. He is talking at the heavenly level, and they are listening at the earthly level. But because the one God created both **heaven** and earth, and because the point of Jesus' work is precisely to bring the life of heaven to earth, the misunderstandings are, in that sense, 'natural'. Jesus, asking for a drink, tells the woman that *she* should have asked *him* for one. She is, of course, bound to think he means it in the ordinary sense.

The clue that he doesn't is found in the phrase '*living* water'. That's the regular phrase people used in Jesus' world for what we call 'running' water – water in a stream or river, rather than a pool or well, water that's more likely to be fresh and clean than water that's been standing around getting stagnant. But here the double meaning kicks into operation; because of course Jesus isn't referring to physical water, whether still or moving. He is referring to the new **life** that he is offering to anyone: as this conversation shows, anyone at all, no matter what their gender, their geography, their racial or moral background.

What Jesus says about this 'living water' makes it clear that he's talking about something quite different, something for which all the water on earth is just a signpost, a pointer. Not only will the water he's offering quench your thirst so that you'll never be thirsty again. It will become a spring bubbling up inside you, refreshing you with the new life which is coming into the world with Jesus and which is the life of the whole new world God is making (verse 14). Later, Jesus will say something like this again, and John will explain that he's referring to the **spirit** (7.37–39). Here the promise remains teasing, cryptic and puzzling.

But it's enough for the woman. She doesn't know exactly what he's talking about, but she wants to know more. What other meanings she was thinking of, we cannot now fathom. But she's in for a shock – as is everyone who starts to take Jesus seriously. He has living water to offer all right, but when you start to drink it it will change every area of your life.

JOHN 4.16–26

Jesus and the Woman

¹⁶'Well then,' said Jesus to the woman, 'go and call your husband and come here.'

¹⁷'I haven't got a husband,' replied the woman.

'You're telling me you haven't got a husband!' replied Jesus. [18]'The fact is, you've had five husbands, and the one you've got now isn't your husband. You were speaking the truth!'

[19]'Well, sir,' replied the woman, 'I can see you're a prophet . . . [20]Our ancestors worshipped on this mountain. And you say that in Jerusalem is the place where people ought to worship.'

[21]'Believe me, woman,' replied Jesus, 'the time is coming when you won't worship the father on this mountain or in Jerusalem. [22]You worship what you don't know. We worship what we do know; salvation, you see, is indeed from the Jews. [23]But the time is coming – indeed, it's here already! – when true worshippers will worship the father in spirit and in truth. Yes; that's the kind of worshippers the father is looking for. [24]God is spirit, and those who worship him must worship in spirit and in truth.'

[25]'I know that Messiah is coming,' said the woman, 'the one they call "the anointed". When he comes, he'll tell us everything.'

[26]'I'm the one – the one speaking to you right now,' said Jesus.

A friend of mine described the reaction when he went home, as a young teenager, and announced to his mother that he'd become a Christian.

Alarmed, she thought he'd joined some kind of cult.

'They've brainwashed you!' she said.

He was ready with the right answer.

'If you'd seen what was in my brain,' he replied, 'you'd realize it needed washing!'

Of course, he hadn't been brainwashed. In fact, again and again – and this was certainly the case with my friend – when people bring their lives, their outer lives and inner lives, into the light of Jesus the **Messiah**, things begin to come clear.

If anything, it's our surrounding culture that brainwashes us, persuading us in a thousand subtle ways that the present world is the only one there is. This is seldom argued. Rather, a mood is created in which it seems so much easier to go with the flow. That's what happens in brainwashing. What the **gospel** does is to administer a sharp jolt, to shine a bright light, to kick-start the brain, and the moral sensibility, into working properly for the first time.

Often, when this begins to happen, the reaction is just like it was with the woman of Samaria. Intrigued by Jesus' offer of 'living water', she asks to have some – not realizing that if you want to take Jesus up on his offer of running, pure water, bubbling up inside you, you will have to get rid of the stale, mouldy, stagnant water you've been living off all this time. In her case it was her married life – or rather, her unmarried life.

Jesus saw straight to the heart of what was going on. (Remember how he did the same to Nathanael (1.47–49), with a similar result?)

The woman has had a life composed of one emotional upheaval after another, with enough husbands coming and going to keep all the gossips in the village chattering for weeks. We assume that her various marriages ended in divorce, whether legal or informal, and not with the death of the men in question. We don't know whether she was equally sinned against as sinning. We don't know what emotional traumas in her background may have made it harder for her to form lasting emotional bonds, though it seems as though the traumas she was at least partly responsible for will have made it harder and harder for her each time. But she knew her life was in a mess, and she knew that Jesus knew.

Her reaction to this is a classic example of what every pastor and evangelist knows only too well. Put your finger on the sore spot, and people will at once start talking about something else. And the best subject for distracting attention from morality is, of course, religion.

I can hear the voices, again and again.

'Well, we used to go to the church in town, but then my aunt said we should go with her, and then I didn't like the minister's wife, and now we've stopped going altogether.'

'Of course, my mother was Catholic and my father was Protestant, so I grew up not really knowing who I was.'

'Well, I was brought up a Methodist, but then my sister and I used to go to the Baptist youth club, and then when we moved away I never really knew anyone.'

And here, two thousand years ago, the same tone of voice.

'I was brought up to think that this mountain, here in Samaria, was God's holy mountain. But you Jews think yours is the right one.' Implication: we can't both be right, maybe nobody knows, maybe nothing is that certain, and maybe (the hidden punchline of the argument) the morality we were taught is equally uncertain.

They are all excuses, and they're all irrelevant. God and the church aren't the same thing. God's claim on every human life – and God's offer of a new kind of human **life** for all who give up the stagnant water and come to him for the living variety – is absolute, and can't be avoided by questions about which church people think they should go to, any more than Jesus' claim on this woman's moral conscience could be avoided by the debate, already hundreds of years old, as to whether Mount Zion, in Jerusalem, or Mount Gerizim, in Samaria, was the true holy mountain.

In fact, part of the point of Jesus' mission, to bring the life of **heaven** to birth on earth, was that from now on holy mountains wouldn't matter that much. This wasn't a new insight. When Solomon dedicated the **Temple** a thousand years before, he was quite clear that heaven itself wasn't big enough for God, so that one single building couldn't hope to contain him. Holy buildings, and holy mountains, are at best signposts to the real thing. If they become substitutes for it, you're in trouble. That way lies idolatry, the worship of something that isn't God as if it were.

Because, as Jesus emphasizes here, the true and living God isn't contained geographically or architecturally. He is **spirit**: not the kind of spirit that abhors the physical world (he made it, after all), but the kind that, as we say, transcends it, rather as the author and producer of a play 'transcend' the action on stage – even though, in this case, it seems as though the author has himself come to play the leading role.

All this is too much for the woman. She certainly wouldn't have enjoyed Jesus reaffirming that 'salvation comes from the Jews' (verse 22), but she probably couldn't make much sense of the idea that true worship would one day have nothing to do with territory and everything to do with spirituality and truth. (Come to think of it, a lot of people today have trouble with that, too.)

So she tries a different tack. Perhaps this will put the stranger off.

'One day the **Messiah** will come,' she says brightly. 'Why don't we wait till then? He'll make it all clear.'

That is, of course, the equivalent of a football player kicking the ball enthusiastically towards his own net, without realizing that the goalkeeper isn't there.

'That's me,' says Jesus.

And he goes on saying it. Whenever people come round to the key questions, and say, 'If only someone would come and sort it all out!' then there he is. 'That's me.' Waiting to do what he does best.

JOHN 4.27–42

Sower and Reaper Rejoice Together

[27]Just then Jesus' disciples came up. They were astonished that he was talking with a woman; but nobody said 'What did you want?' or 'Why were you talking with her?' [28]So the woman left her water-jar, went into the town and spoke to the people.

[29]'Come on!' she said. 'Come and see a man who told me everything I ever did! You don't think he can be the Messiah, do you?'

[30]So they left the town and were coming out to him.

[31]Meanwhile the disciples were nagging him.

'Come on, rabbi!' they were saying. 'You must have something to eat!'

[32]'I've got food to eat that you know nothing about,' he said.

[33]'Nobody's brought him anything to eat, have they?' said the disciples to one another.

³⁴'My food', replied Jesus, 'is to do the will of the one who sent me, and to finish his work! ³⁵Don't you have a saying, "Another four months, then comes harvest"? Well, let me tell you, raise your eyes and see! The fields are white! It's harvest time already! ³⁶The reaper earns his pay, and gathers crops for the life of God's coming age, so that sower and reaper can celebrate together. ³⁷This is where that saying comes true, "One sows, another reaps". ³⁸I sent you to reap what you didn't work for. Others did the hard work, and you've come into the results.'

³⁹Several Samaritans from that town believed in Jesus because of what the woman said in evidence about him, 'He told me everything I did.' ⁴⁰So when the Samaritans came to him, they asked him to stay with them. And he stayed there two days.

⁴¹Many more believed because of what he said.

⁴²'We believe, too,' they said to the woman, 'but it's no longer because of what you told us. We've heard him ourselves! We know that he really is the one! He's the saviour of the world!'

I was telephoned this morning by a colleague who was writing a piece about George Frideric Handel's masterpiece, *Messiah*. We agreed that it has a unique place in the affection not only of Christians, and of serious music-lovers, but of a far wider public. Among the many remarkable things about the work is the fact that the early performances raised money for charity, and that ever since then vast sums have been raised through performances great and small, professional and amateur. Somehow, wherever in the world this music is played, the message has gone home that people in need can be helped, indeed saved, by the story of Jesus.

One of the most extraordinary things about the way Handel composed *Messiah* is what a short time it took him. Granted, some of the tunes were taken from his own earlier works; Handel always believed that if a tune was worth hearing once it was probably worth hearing twice. The work was completed in a few weeks of sustained activity, during which he frequently went for long periods without food, carried along by the music, which he could scarcely get down on to paper fast enough. He spoke afterwards of that time as a wonderful, exalted, heavenly vision.

That kind of exhilaration, it seems, is given only rarely. But it must have been something like that that Jesus was referring to when he said, explaining why he wasn't hungry, that he had food to eat which his followers didn't know about. They, of course, thought he meant that someone else had secretly brought him some food. Like the woman when Jesus was talking about water, their understanding is staying on the ordinary, earthbound level.

Jesus, however, is on tiptoe with excitement at what has just happened. From the woman's point of view, the conversation has thrown her into happy confusion: she seems to regard Jesus as a cross between a fortune-teller and a **Messiah**, but at least it's given her the energy to go and tell other people about him. For Jesus, the turn the conversation has taken, and the woman's reaction, have shown him that here, outside the boundaries of the chosen people, away from Jerusalem itself, there is a spiritual hunger which, in however muddled a fashion, is ready to hear what he has to say.

As a result he can see, in his mind's eye, the fields of corn turning white, ready for harvest. Growing up among country people, he would instinctively know the rhythms of agricultural life, the moments of excitement, and the small but profound proverbs which cluster around sowing and reaping. Here are two of them. 'Another four months, then it's harvest time'; in other words, there's always a time lag between sowing and reaping. Not so, says Jesus: in this case, there's no time lag at all! No sooner sown than reaped! Don't delay, it's harvest time already! And again, 'One sows, another reaps'; yes, he says, and the sowers have done their work and you are the reapers! You haven't done the hard work, but you're going to get the reward nonetheless.

The thought of a brand new field opening up for the harvest of the **gospel** was exciting then, and when the same thing happens today it remains exhilarating. It is even more exciting, in fact, than the thought of a good harvest out in the fields; here, as verse 36 insists, sower and reaper may celebrate together. Perhaps Jesus is thinking of **John the Baptist** as the sower, and himself and his followers as the reapers. Or perhaps he is thinking, not just of John, but of the whole sequence of prophets and righteous Israelites up to John. But the point is that the moment has come, the moment of fulfilment, the moment of harvest. And the unlikely midday conversation with a puzzled and outcast woman has made Jesus realize it in a new way.

When were you last so excited about something that you didn't need to eat? For that matter, when were you last looking, with the eyes of Jesus, at the harvest waiting to be gathered? Might those two questions perhaps have anything to do with each other?

The way the passage ends is worth pondering deeply. Here is a woman who, a matter of an hour or so before, had been completely trapped in a life of immorality, as a social outcast. There was no way backwards or forwards for her; all she could do was to eke out a daily existence and make sure she went to the well at the time of day when there would be nobody there to sneer or mock. Now she has become the first evangelist to the Samaritan people. Before any of Jesus' own followers could do it, she has told them that he is the Messiah. And then, as they have come to see Jesus for themselves, they have become convinced.

Indeed, they have given Jesus a title which, as they may have known, the emperor in far-away Rome had begun to use for himself: saviour of the world. John frequently shows us how people misunderstand what Jesus is saying, but he also shows us that sometimes they can break through, with little or no help, to a statement of truth so profound that it could stand as a summary of all that John himself is trying to tell us. Jesus is indeed the world's saviour. That is part of the task and role of Israel's Messiah. Salvation may indeed be 'from the Jews' (4.22), but part of the point of it is that salvation is designed to reach outside Judaism to embrace the world. Now, with this incident in Samaria, that process has begun.

JOHN 4.43–54

The Official's Son

⁴³After the two days in Samaria, Jesus went off from there to Galilee. ⁴⁴Jesus himself gave evidence, after all, that a prophet isn't honoured in his own country. ⁴⁵So when he came to Galilee, the Galileans welcomed him. They had seen all the things he had done in Jerusalem at the festival, they having been at the festival themselves.

⁴⁶So he went once more to Cana in Galilee, where he had turned the water into wine.

There was a royal official in Capernaum whose son was ill. ⁴⁷He heard that Jesus had come from Judaea into Galilee, and he went to him and asked him to come down and heal his son, since he was at the point of death.

⁴⁸'Unless you see signs and miracles,' replied Jesus, 'you won't ever believe.'

⁴⁹'Sir,' replied the official, 'come down before my child dies!'

⁵⁰'Off you go!' said Jesus. 'Your son will live!'

The man believed the word which Jesus had spoken to him, and he set off. ⁵¹But while he was still on his way down to Capernaum, his servants met him with the news that his son was alive and well.

⁵²So he asked them what time he had begun to get better.

'Yesterday afternoon, about one o'clock,' they said. 'That's when the fever left him.'

⁵³So the father knew that it had happened at the very moment when Jesus had said to him, 'Your son will live!' He himself believed, and so did all his household.

⁵⁴This was now the second sign Jesus did, when he came out of Judaea into Galilee.

Remember the treasure hunt and the clues? (Think back to 2.1–12.) Here is the second clue, the second 'sign'. But this time there's something strange about it. There's a bit of a cloud hanging over the whole story. Something is not quite right, not quite as straightforward as the final scene in Samaria.

It's almost as though, while we're running the treasure hunt, we discover that several of the competitors have become more interested in the clues for their own sake than in following them and discovering the treasure. After all, the clues have been written in clever little rhymes; some of the participants seem to be keen on poems, so they are reading them to each other in appreciation, forgetting that the point of them is to lead them towards the actual goal.

Or, to change the picture, imagine a town planner designing a new set of road signs to get people round the streets in the quickest and easiest fashion. The town is old, famous and beautiful, and nothing but very fine and well-designed signs will do for such a setting. But when the signs are put up, you discover that everyone is stopping and getting out of their cars to stand and admire the signs. Instead of the traffic flowing smoothly by, it's getting clogged up worse than before.

Let's put it yet another way, this time in terms of the big picture which John is showing us. The **Word** has become flesh. But supposing people admire the flesh so much that they forget about the Word?

That, it seems, is the danger Jesus is now facing – and will continue to face through the next seven chapters, as the sequence of 'signs' unfolds before our eyes. The question we must face is not only what was going on in Jesus' ministry, but whether we ourselves are learning to make proper and appropriate use of the 'signs' that we are given.

The problem begins when Jesus goes back to his home territory of Galilee. This passage is one of the few in John's **gospel** which takes place in Galilee (the others are the call of Philip and Nathanael (1.43–51), the opening 'sign' at Cana in Galilee (2.1–12), and the multiplication of loaves (chapter 6)). Unlike the other gospels, most of the action in this one takes place in Jerusalem. Verses 44–45 may then seem a bit puzzling: it looks as though John is first saying that prophets aren't honoured in their own country, and then that the Galileans, Jesus' own countrymen and countrywomen, welcomed him, remembering the things he'd done in Jerusalem. So did they honour him, after all?

Yes and no. Verse 48 is the clue. Jesus is anxious that the welcome in Galilee, such as it is, is superficial. They are sitting down to read the clues rather than following them to the treasure. They are taking photographs of the road signs rather than driving where the signs tell them to. They are wanting a **Messiah** who will perform **miracles** to order, rather than moving on to the real **faith** which will grasp Jesus' hidden identity, the **Word** dwelling in the flesh.

John tells us that this is the second 'sign' that Jesus did, and from now on he leaves us to do our own counting. But what was the proper response? Why did Jesus do signs if he didn't want people to follow him for the wrong reasons?

The proper response was the one he got from the official in verses 50 and 53. The man *believed the word* which Jesus spoke to him. The fact that he set off home, without insisting that Jesus come with him from Cana, up in the hills, to Capernaum, down by the lake, is a clear indication that his faith didn't happen because he saw miracles, but because he heard Jesus' word. When the word was confirmed by the actual healing, taking place at the same moment but at a distance, he and his whole family believed. The word Jesus had spoken had become flesh.

The distinction between believing because we've seen something and believing on the strength of Jesus' words remains important throughout the gospel. It reaches its final dramatic statement in Jesus' gentle rebuke to Thomas in 20.29: 'Have you believed because you've seen? Blessed are those who haven't seen, and yet believe!'

This is the challenge the gospel presents to us today. We are not invited to believe in an abstract idea, or a nebulous feeling, or an indefinable spiritual experience. We are invited to believe in the Word become flesh. But genuine faith is always seeking the Word hidden in the flesh, not using the Word simply as a way of getting at the flesh. As John's story unfolds, we are again and again reminded that, if on the one hand 'God loved the world so much' (3.16), this is not because our life must remain bounded by the present world. When the world is embraced by God in his love, this happens so that we who live in the present world, dark and corrupt as it now is, may learn to love in return the God who has loved us.

Let the clues lead you to the treasure. Let the signs lead you out of the traffic jam. Let the flesh lead you to the Word. Hear, and believe.

JOHN 5.1–9a

The Healing of the Disabled Man

¹After this there was a Jewish festival, and Jesus went up to Jerusalem.

²In Jerusalem, near the Sheep Gate, there is a pool which is called, in Hebrew, Bethesda. It has five porticoes, ³where several sick people were lying. They were blind, lame and paralysed.

⁵There was a man who had been there, in the same sick state, for thirty-eight years. ⁶Jesus saw him lying there, and knew that he had been there a long time already.

'Do you want to get well?' he asked him.

[7]'Well, sir,' the sick man replied, 'I don't have anyone to put me into the pool when the water gets stirred up. While I'm on my way there, someone else gets down before me.'

[8]'Get up,' said Jesus, 'pick up your mattress and walk!'

[9]At once the man was healed. He picked up his mattress and walked.

There were two small boys playing in the overgrown garden. The old man who lived in the big house had been ill for many weeks, and though nurses and doctors came and went to the house nobody seemed to bother about what happened in the garden. So the brothers had quietly taken it over.

They didn't know what to do with the tennis court. They had never seen anyone playing tennis, but the markings on the ground suggested it was for some kind of game. The net hung slack in the middle of the court, and since the only ball they had was a football, they had invented a game of kicking the ball over the net to each other and trying to land it within the lines on the other side. It more or less worked, but was not the most exciting ball game ever invented.

One day the old man's son came from abroad to visit his father. Looking from the upstairs window down the long garden, he saw the boys playing their made-up game. He smiled. Going to a cupboard, he collected an armful of tennis equipment. The boys were alarmed when they saw him coming down the garden. But he wasn't angry.

'Wouldn't you like to play the real thing?'

'What's the real thing?'

'Tennis, of course! Here, I'll show you.'

And within minutes he had swept leaves off the court, tightened the net, equipped the boys with rackets, and begun to teach them the difficult but far more rewarding game that the court was built for.

The pool of Bethesda was a well-known place of healing. It was in Jerusalem itself, just to the north of the **Temple** Mount area. The original site has been excavated by archaeologists, and if you go to Jerusalem you can see it for yourself. But it wasn't just a Jewish healing place. The evidence suggests that pagans, too, regarded it as a sacred site. At one stage it was dedicated to the healing god Asclepius.

The way it worked seems to have been like this. The waters in the pool would bubble up periodically; when that happened, the first person to get in would be healed. Some people reckoned that the bubbling water was caused by an angel. (The reason there is no 'verse 4' in this passage is that several ancient copies of the **gospel** have an extra verse at that point, explaining all this; but most of the oldest and best copies haven't got it.)

But the shrine didn't seem particularly successful. Clearly, the man Jesus found lying there had made a way of life out of his long wait for healing. Jesus' question to him is, perhaps, quite pointed: do you really *want* to get better, or are you now quite happy to eke out your days lounging around here with the feeble excuse that someone else always gets in first? The whole scene, with its legends and its pagan associations, was like the two boys playing football on a tennis court. The place spoke of the possibility of miraculous healing, of the remote chance of divine healing; but it was at best spasmodic, and at worst an idle dream.

Then along comes the one who, John has been telling us, is the true son of the true God. In a flash, he does what the pool stood for but what it hadn't been doing very successfully. As with the official's son in the previous paragraph, a word is all it takes, in this case a command to get up, pick up the mattress and walk. We aren't even told that the man 'believed', but clearly he must have done or he wouldn't have obeyed Jesus' order. He now finds himself launched on the much harder, but much more satisfying, way of life that goes with no longer being a cripple.

As with many of the gospel stories, particularly in John, what Jesus does fulfils the hopes and longings of the Jewish world, expressed as they were in various ways, not least the great festivals (verse 1). Here, however, Jesus seems to be fulfilling the hopes and half-formed beliefs of the pagan world as well. Part of the point of the gospel is that, if 'salvation is of the Jews', and if Jesus is now bringing that salvation, it must spread out *from* the Jews to embrace the wider world. The pagan shrine points dimly to the healing that Jesus was bringing, rather as the strange game of football-in-a-tennis-court points to the game the court was made for.

Paganism looks at the world of creation and tries to harness forces within it for its own ends. The healing that Jesus offers is the reality that the created world was waiting for, the beginning of new creation. The salvation that the **son of God** brings when he comes into the world is the new day that, had they but known it, Israel and the world had been longing for.

In view of the rest of the chapter (see particularly verses 25–29), we may be allowed to see a hint in verse 8 of what that new creation will look like. When Jesus says 'Get up!' the word is one regularly used in the New Testament to describe the **resurrection**. Here is part of the inner secret of Jesus' work. He isn't trying to use one force within the existing creation to put right something else that's gone wrong within the same old creation. He is bringing a new **life**, a new creation. It bursts through into the present world, bringing healing and new possibilities.

And the old creation realizes – like the boys beginning to play tennis – that this is what had been intended all along. No wonder people found it disturbing. No wonder – as we shall see presently – they even found it threatening and scandalous.

The word 'sign' doesn't occur in this passage. By now John expects us to be counting for ourselves.

JOHN 5.9b-18

God's Son Breaks the Sabbath!

⁹ᵇThe day all this happened was a sabbath. ¹⁰So the Judaeans confronted the man who had been healed.

'It's the sabbath!' they said. 'You shouldn't be carrying your mattress!'

¹¹'Well,' he replied, 'the man who cured me told me to pick up my mattress and walk!'

¹²'Oh, really?' they said. 'And who is this man, who told you to pick it up and walk?'

¹³But the man who'd been healed didn't know who it was. Jesus had gone away, and the place was crowded.

¹⁴After this Jesus found the man in the Temple.

'Look!' he said. 'You're better again! Don't sin any more, or something worse might happen to you!'

¹⁵The man went off and told the Judaeans that it was Jesus who had healed him. ¹⁶That was why the Judaeans began to persecute Jesus, because he did these things on the sabbath.

¹⁷This was Jesus' response to them.

'My father,' he said, 'is going on working, and so am I!'

¹⁸So for this reason the Judaeans were all the more eager to kill him, because he not only broke the sabbath, but spoke of God as his own father, making himself equal to God.

I woke up to hear a voice speaking a language I didn't understand. Where was I? What was going on?

A dim light from the other side of the room reminded me. I was at the conference. I was sharing a room with a colleague from the university, a distinguished Indian scholar, who taught Hinduism.

It was four o'clock in the morning where we were, and he was on the telephone to his wife. It was already seven o'clock in Montreal, and she would be getting up with the children. He wanted her to know we were safe.

He came off the phone. I chided him. 'Come on! It's four in the morning! It's time for rest!'

'No,' he said, 'it's time to wake up – at least it is at home! My wife has to get off to work soon and I had to speak to her.'

The point of this passage is that Jesus and his Judaean opponents are working in two different time zones. Not geographical time zones, of course; ancient travel wasn't fast enough for people to notice such things, and since they didn't have electronic communications the issue doesn't seem to have been raised. Rather, they were in what you might call different *theological* time zones. Basically, the Judaeans think it's still time for rest, but Jesus is wide awake, and has already started the business of the day.

The issue concerned the **sabbath**. As we discover in the Old Testament, one of its original purposes was to highlight the seventh day as the time when the creator God rested from his work in making the world. Week by week, the **law**-observant Jews kept a strict day without work – defining quite carefully what 'work' might include so there would be no doubt.

Jesus, however, seems systematically to have continued doing things on the sabbath that could be understood – and were understood by some at least of his opponents – as deliberate 'work'. After all, in the present case he didn't have to heal the man that day. He'd waited nearly forty years to be healed; another day wouldn't have hurt him. But Jesus seems deliberately to have chosen to do it that day. And, though what Jesus himself had done was hardly 'work' – all he'd done was to issue a command – what he'd told the man to do, to carry his mattress, certainly was.

Jesus' explanation, like that of my friend at the conference, was that he was living in a different time zone. His father was at work, and it was important for him to be as well. What could he have meant?

The heart of it seems to be Jesus' belief that Israel's God was then and there in the process of launching the *new creation*. And somehow this new creation was superseding the old one. Its timescale was taking precedence. God was healing the sorry, sick old world, and though there might come a time for rest (when Jesus' own work was finished, maybe: see 19.28–30), at the moment it was time for the work of new creation to go forward. Especially, from John's point of view, if the 'signs' correspond in some way to the 'days' of the new creation.

We can hardly expect such a viewpoint to be popular among the law-observant Judaeans. Here we meet the sharpest opposition so far. As the 'signs' build up, so the reaction to them becomes fiercer; people begin to realize just what it will cost to follow where these signs are pointing.

The 'Judaeans', by the way, were the inhabitants of Judaea, the southern part of the country. The word is the same as for 'the Jews', but that can't be what John means, since of course Jesus and his followers, and the man he healed by the pool, were all Jews as well. Elsewhere he seems to use the word quite carefully to mean 'the Jews who live in Judaea as opposed to Galilee' (see, e.g., 7.1). Here, in fact, we have the beginning of that violent opposition to Jesus, centred in Jerusalem itself, which would eventually explode in a capital charge (11.47–53), and in Jesus' arrest and death.

If Jesus' work of healing and new creation was going forward, what was holding it up? Not just opposition, but also sin. There is a dark mystery here, because in the present case Jesus implies that the crippled man had got into his present condition because of his own sin (verse 14), but four chapters later Jesus also insists that the condition of the man born blind had nothing to do with anyone's sin (9.1–3). It seems that some sicknesses may be related to some sins, but you can't and shouldn't deduce the one from the other. (I had a letter two days ago from someone who saw all too clearly how sin has caused her serious illness; but I know many sick people for whom that would be an absurd conclusion, and indeed many cheerful and healthy sinners.)

We see here, in fact, the expansion and outworking of the short, sad statement in the **gospel** Prologue (1.10–11): 'He came to his own, and his own didn't accept him.' They were not ready for new creation, for the living **Word** of God to come to them with new things to say. They were living in the old time zone, and were angry with Jesus for, as it were, waking them up too soon. The battle of the time zones will continue until it reaches its climax on the cross.

This battle still continues today, though in another form. With Jesus' **resurrection**, God's new-creation project is launched upon the whole world. People still react angrily to it. Where are the followers of Jesus today who are prepared to say 'Jesus is at work, and so am I?'

JOHN 5.19–29

The Coming Judgment

[19]So Jesus made this response to them.

'I'm telling you the solemn truth,' he said. 'The son can do nothing by himself. He can only do what he sees the father doing. Whatever the father does, the son does too, and in the same way. [20]The father loves the son, you see, and shows him all the things that he's doing. Yes: he will show him even greater things than these, and that'll amaze you! [21]For, just as the father raises the dead and gives them life, in the same way the son gives life to anyone he chooses.

[22]'The father doesn't judge anyone, you see; he has handed over all judgment to the son, [23]so that everyone should honour the son just as

they honour the father. Anyone who doesn't honour the son doesn't honour the father who sent him.

²⁴'I'm telling you the solemn truth: anyone who hears my word, and believes in the one who sent me, has the life of God's coming age. Such a person won't come into judgment; they will have passed out of death into life. ²⁵I'm telling you the solemn truth: the time is coming – in fact, it's here already! – when the dead will hear the voice of God's son, and those who hear it will live. ²⁶You see, just as the father has life in himself, in the same way he has given the son the privilege of having life in himself. ²⁷He has even given him authority to pass judgment, because he is the son of man.

²⁸'Don't be surprised at this. The time is coming, you see, when everyone in the tombs will hear his voice. ²⁹They will come out – those who have done good, to the resurrection of life, and those who have done evil, to the resurrection of judgment.'

I spent two hours this morning reading part of my oldest son's doctoral dissertation. It isn't on a subject I know anything about, but I was checking to see if I could catch any last-minute typographical mistakes, and to get the feel of how the sentences worked, and whether it all seemed to make sense.

We often talk about writing, since we both do quite a lot of it, and I realize that in an informal way he has been, as it were, unofficially apprenticed to me. He has watched me writing over the years; he has his own natural aptitude, and a different style as well as subject matter; but we both take quiet pleasure in working on things side by side. Simultaneously, my younger son is conducting a short-term project under my direction, and there the sense of apprenticeship is even more marked.

This is rare in the modern Western world, but there are still plenty of places where it is the normal and expected thing for sons to follow fathers into the family business. (In my family I was the first son for six generations to break away from just such a pattern.) And, particularly where the business involves working at a skilled trade with one's hands, apprenticeship means literally being side by side, with the son watching every move that the father makes and learning to do it in exactly the same way. That is how many traditional skills are handed down from generation to generation, often over hundreds of years.

Verses 19–23 seem to be almost a **parable**, a story about how sons can be apprenticed to their fathers; though of course the particular father and son here are God and Jesus. Jesus is explaining more fully how it is that Israel's God is working in a new way, and how he, Jesus, is watching carefully to see how it's being done, so as to do it alongside the father and in keeping with his style and plan. And the most astonishing thing the father is doing, which, like everything else, he is showing the son so that the son can then do it with him and on his behalf, is this: he is giving **life** to the dead. The hint about **resurrection** earlier in the chapter, and the riddle about it in chapter 2 (verses 19–22), are now coming into clearer focus.

It was already a popular Jewish belief in Jesus' day that God would raise the dead. The later **rabbis** made it an article of **faith**, but most Jews already believed it anyway. There would come a day, they believed, when God – who, as the creator, was committed to bringing justice to his world – would put everything to rights. This would involve bringing all evil to scrutiny and condemnation, and vindicating all who had followed God's way. And it was no use imagining that this condemnation and vindication would take place in some otherworldly setting. God the creator would bring people back into bodily life, to face the consequences of their evil deeds, or share the rewards of their righteous ones. That, at any rate, was what the book of Daniel had said (12.2), and that statement was very influential in the first century.

What Jesus is now saying is that with his coming and public ministry *this work of raising the dead has already begun*. This is central to the work that he's watching the father do, and that he is doing alongside him. It will come to an astonishing peak, within this story, when he raises Lazarus from the dead (chapter 11); then it will reach its full flowering when Jesus himself goes through death and out the other side into the full splendour of resurrection life (chapters 20 and 21). The present passage is preparing us for all that.

But Jesus is now supplying the secret that helps us to see what is going on when people, during the course of his ministry, see and hear what he's doing and come to believe in him, to believe that he is indeed the **Word** made flesh. This is the extra, hidden truth inside the statement in the Prologue that anyone who receives him, who believes in his name, gains the right to be called God's child. This is the secret truth inside the promise of new birth (1.12–13; 3.1–8).

Those who are born from above in this way are not just receiving a new spiritual experience, the life of God's **spirit** welling up within them like 'living water' (4.14). They are passing from death to life. The **miracle** of resurrection is taking place inside them, so that, when they finally die physically, that event will be irrelevant to the new life they already have. What God does in the present he will complete in the future, when the present 'resurrection', the new birth during the present life, finally produces the future bodily resurrection that will correspond to Jesus' own.

What the father has given to the son, then, is the right to execute judgment on his behalf. The explanation Jesus gives here ('because he is the **son of man**, verse 27) draws on the ancient Jewish picture of 'one like a son of man' in Daniel 7, who is given authority over the world, and particularly to bring God's just judgment on the forces of tyranny and evil that have oppressed God's people. You could put it like this: God has longed to put the world to rights; now, with his apprentice son on the job, he is doing so at last. But bringing new creation to birth can only be done if the evil that has corrupted the old creation is named, shamed and dealt with. That's what judgment is all about.

How does this faith help us to live in a world where tyranny and injustice are still rampant?

JOHN 5.30–38

The Evidence in Support of Jesus

[30]'I can't do anything on my own authority,' Jesus went on. 'I judge on the basis of what I hear. And my judgment is just, because I'm not trying to carry out my own wishes, but the wishes of the one who sent me.

[31]'If I give evidence about myself, my evidence isn't true. [32]There is someone else who gives evidence about me, and I know that the evidence he brings about me is true. [33]You sent messengers to John, and he gave evidence about the truth. [34]Not that I need evidence from human beings; but I'm saying this so that you may be saved.

[35]'John was a burning, bright lamp, and you were happy to celebrate in his light for a while. [36]But I have greater evidence on my side than that of John. The works which the father has given me to complete – these works, which I'm doing, will provide evidence about me, evidence that the father has sent me. [37]And the father who sent me has given evidence about me. You've never heard his voice; you've never seen his form. [38]What's more, you haven't got his word abiding in you, because you don't believe in the one he sent.'

'He would say that, wouldn't he?'

The prosecution lawyer had just informed the defendant that a notable person, who had been implicated in the shady goings-on, had made a statement to the police denying all the allegations the defendant had made against him.

The defendant's answer became famous. If someone gives evidence, however seriously, in their own defence, many today will just shrug their shoulders and say the same. 'He would, wouldn't he?'

It wasn't much different in the ancient world. To prove your point, you need witnesses. Evidence. People who will stand up and put their own reputation on the line to back you.

Frequently in John's **gospel** we have the sense that we are spectators in a court of law. John keeps on talking about 'evidence', or, as it's sometimes translated, 'testimony' or 'witness'. At this stage, it looks as though Jesus is on trial, though it's not clear what the charge is. The 'evidence' he's talking about isn't just in relation to his supposed breaking of the **sabbath** in healing the man by the pool. It goes wider than that. In fact, it also goes much further back: to the very beginning of the gospel, when we are told that **John the Baptist** came 'to give evidence about the light' (1.7), and that in his evidence he insisted that he wasn't the **Messiah** himself, but that Jesus was (1.19–20, 32–34).

But now we seem to be offered evidence which is greater even than that of John the Baptist. Jesus quickly disposes of any suggestion that he is simply talking about himself; verse 33 anticipates the charge 'Well, you would say that, wouldn't you?' This is especially interesting because people often suggest that in John's gospel Jesus goes around making striking claims about himself. The reality is more subtle. Here Jesus goes around asking people to look at the evidence of their eyes.

Not that John the Baptist wasn't important. Verses 33–35 form an eloquent testimony to the power and truth of John's career. The people of Israel were glad to think that they had a real prophet speaking to them in their own day; but they had not, so far, been prepared to look where John pointed, and to see in Jesus the one for whom John was preparing the way.

In fact, though, the greatest evidence of all is that which the father himself provides. How can you tell that Jesus is really watching the one true God, as an apprentice son watches his father in the workplace, and is copying him all down the line? Because that's how he is able to do the extraordinary things he is doing. John has only, so far, told us about three remarkable things (the 'signs') that Jesus has done, but he has already implied that there were plenty of others (e.g. 2.24). When he sums up the whole book, he declares that there were indeed so many others that you would never be able to write them all down (20.30; 21.25). Those who were with Jesus, watching what he did, had the evidence before them; they should have been able to make up their minds. Was he the Messiah? Was he from God? And, behind all this, was he somehow *embodying* the living God in himself?

The problem is that the members of the jury, watching and considering their verdict, were not in a fit condition to understand the evidence before them. In verse 37 we see the beginning of Jesus' charge against his contemporaries, those who watched it all going on and turned away in disbelief. In fact, we see the beginning of what turns out to be the alternative 'trial' in the gospel. It isn't really Jesus who is on trial. He, after all, is the judge, who will carry out God's just judgment (verse 30). It is the people who are watching, listening and then ignoring him. They are the ones on trial.

But they don't know the God they profess to believe in. They haven't truly seen him or heard him. His word finds no place in them. Over the next few chapters, this warning note will build up until, with sorrow, John reports in chapter 12 that by the time Jesus made his last journey to Jerusalem the people at large were completely set in their minds against him – and were thus, themselves, incurring judgment.

The worrying thing about this is that it wasn't just a problem in Jesus' day. John sees this as a problem that the whole world faces. Once the story of Jesus has been told, the jury is out – on the hearers, not on Jesus himself. God has given evidence in Jesus' favour, the only evidence which ultimately counts: that is part of the meaning of Jesus' **resurrection**. The question is, what will we do with Jesus? When the truly just judgment comes, will we be among those who are weighed by the court and found wanting?

JOHN 5.39–47

Jesus and Moses

> [39]'You study the Bible', Jesus continued, 'because you suppose that you'll discover the life of God's coming age in it. In fact, it's the Bible which gives evidence about me! [40]But you won't come to me so that you can have life.
>
> [41]'I'm not accepting glory from human beings; [42]but I know that you haven't got the love of God within you. [43]I have come in the name of my father, and you won't receive me. If someone else comes in his own name, you will receive him! [44]How can you believe, when you receive glory from one another, and you're not looking for the glory which comes from the one and only God?
>
> [45]'Don't think that I'm going to accuse you to the father. There is someone who accuses you, namely Moses, the one you look to in hope! [46]You see, if you'd believed Moses, you would have believed me – because it was me he was writing about. [47]But if you don't believe his writings, how are you going to believe my words?'

You can see it in a class at school. You can see it in a sports team. You can see it in an army barracks. You can see it, in fact, almost anywhere where a peer group builds up and gathers momentum despite the best efforts of those in charge.

The boys who sit at the back of the class are more interested in showing off to those around than in doing what the teacher wants.

The players who are out to boost their own image on the sports field attempt flashy moves which look good at the time but don't score goals. The soldiers with an eye on their colleagues, rather than on their commanding officer, are full of apparent bravado and heroism, but when they face the enemy they don't know what to do.

Now supposing, instead of a teacher, a sports coach or a commanding officer, you have none other than God, the living, patient, loving, wise God, who has called a people to belong to himself so that through them he could reveal his glory to the world. And supposing this people are so pleased with their calling that they spend their time trying to impress each other rather than trying to please God. That is the charge that Jesus, solemnly and sorrowfully, levels against his contemporaries, as he comes to his own and his own don't accept him (1.11).

We can see something of what he meant if we think of the parties that then existed within Judaism. Paul, who had been at the extreme end of the **Pharisee** party, speaks in Galatians of having 'advanced in Judaism beyond my contemporaries, being extremely zealous for my ancestral traditions' (Galatians 1.14). There was, it seems, an unofficial ranking system, a more-zealous-than-thou competition, and the young Saul of Tarsus was near the top of it. And part of the subject matter was the Bible. Master the text, show that you know **Torah** inside out and back to front, and you'll impress the others in the class.

But will you impress God? No, declares Paul in Galatians and elsewhere; no, declares Jesus in this passage. Think back again to the Prologue (1.17): the **law** was given through Moses, but grace and truth came through Jesus the **Messiah**. The law was and is a good thing (we mustn't make the mistake that some early Christians made, of supposing that Jesus and Paul were dismissing the law as a bad thing), but its whole point was not to enable you to look good in your own estimation, or to show off to those around, but to bring you to the Messiah.

The Jewish law told a story which came to its climax in him. It pointed to the ideal for human life, and to God's provision of **sacrifice** for human sin, not so that people could boast of how successfully they'd accomplished it all, but to point to the Messiah, the truly human being (see 19.5), the lamb of God who would take away the sin of the world.

Jesus' charge against his contemporaries is thus that they have been looking at the right book but reading it the wrong way. Those of us who spend our lives poring over the Bible as scholars, preachers and teachers need to take this warning to heart. It is easy to be attracted to the study of the text as an exercise in intellectual brilliance. The Bible is the most fascinating book, or collection of books, in the world, and anyone with a feel for literature, for ideas, for history, for great stories, can become completely absorbed in it. The academic discussions which arise from it can be fascinating, exhilarating and as challenging and stimulating as any other subject in the curriculum. And God wants the best minds to be working on this job. There is yet more light to break out of the Bible, and if this is to happen it needs people to soak themselves in it at every level.

But it is possible to allow the study of the text, and of different interpretations of the text, to become a substitute for allowing the text to bring us into the presence of the living God. It is deceptively easy to know everything about 'the Jewish hope for the Messiah', and not to know the Messiah himself, in person. And it is all too simple – indeed, sometimes our academic institutions and seminaries encourage it – to use our knowledge and intellectual ability to gain status and prestige among our colleagues, or among those who belong to the same part of (or party within) the church as we do. That is as true today as it was in Jesus' day.

This is not to say that we must leave our minds behind when we read the text, and simply have nice warm feelings about Jesus. On the contrary. To read the Bible in the light of Jesus the Messiah demands more thought, not less. But this thought must always be ready to pass into personal knowledge, into adoration, into prayer – and then back again, because there will always be more to study. From scripture to Messiah and back again, and so on to and fro in an upward spiral of understanding. That is the challenge which this passage presented then, and presents to us still.

JOHN 6.1–15

Feeding the Five Thousand

¹After this Jesus went away beside the sea of Galilee, that is, the sea of Tiberias. ²A large crowd followed him, because they saw the signs he was doing in healing the sick. ³Jesus went up into the mountain and sat down there with his disciples. ⁴It was nearly time for the Passover, a Jewish festival.

⁵Jesus looked up and saw a great crowd coming to him.

'Where are we going to buy bread,' he said to Philip, 'so that they can have something to eat?' ⁶(He said this to test him. He himself knew what he intended to do.)

⁷'Even with six months' pay', replied Philip, 'you wouldn't be able to buy enough bread for each of them to have just a little!'

⁸One of his disciples, Andrew, Simon Peter's brother, joined in.

⁹'There's a lad here', he said, 'who's got five barley loaves and two fish. But what use are they with this many people?'

¹⁰'Make the men sit down,' said Jesus.

There was a lot of grass where they were, so the men sat down, about five thousand in all. ¹¹So Jesus took the loaves, gave thanks and gave them to the people sitting down, and then did the same with the fish, as much as they wanted.

¹²When they were satisfied, he called the disciples.

'Collect up the bits and pieces left over,' he said, 'so that we don't lose anything.'

¹³So they collected it up, and filled twelve baskets with broken pieces of the five barley loaves left behind by the people who had eaten.

¹⁴When the people saw the sign that Jesus had done, they said, 'This really is the Prophet, the one who is to come into the world.' ¹⁵So when Jesus realized that they were intending to come and seize him to make him king, he withdrew again, by himself, up the mountain.

When you read detective stories, you quickly learn that what may look like an irrelevant little detail may actually be the clue to discovering who the murderer really is. A good writer will put in all kinds of detail, designed to lead the eye and the mind in several different directions; nothing is there by accident. But somewhere in the middle is the sign that, if only you'd been thinking hard about it at the time, will tell you the secret.

Nothing in John's **gospel** is there by accident. In fact, there is so much detail here, so many lines of thought one might follow up, that it can become bewildering. Unlike a detective story, all the details in John are designed ultimately to come together, rather than to lead us up blind alleys. But the really important thing is to pick up the clues he gives us which point to the big, central things, the places where the deepest meaning is to be found.

This is the second time John has told us of something happening at Passover time; the previous time was when Jesus was in Jerusalem, casting out the traders in the **Temple** (2.13). There will be a third time, when Jesus arrives in Jerusalem for the last time, and then it is so important for John's understanding of what is about to happen that he mentions it three times (11.55; 12.1; 13.1). This is no detective story; John is not trying to keep us guessing. He wants us to understand, as we go along, where it is all going.

So when he draws our attention to the fact that the extraordinary feeding of the crowds took place at Passover time, he is clearly hoping that we will connect it in our minds both with Passover itself – the time when God liberated the children of Israel from Egypt, and led them through the wilderness to the promised land – and with the other

Passover events in the gospel, that is, the 'cleansing of the Temple' on the one hand and Jesus' death and **resurrection** on the other.

The whole of this long sixth chapter of John's gospel is dominated by the theme of Passover, or rather by one aspect of it: the fact that God fed the children of Israel, during their wilderness wanderings, with 'bread from **heaven**'. The story is told in Exodus 16, where the 'manna' is provided by God because the people are grumbling and complaining. Both sides of this story provide part of the important background for John 6.

The chapter opens with this story, which is told in all four gospels, of Jesus' own provision of food for a large crowd out in the wilderness area, across the sea of Galilee and away from towns where food might have been found. As well as providing the starting point for the long discussion of 'the bread from heaven' which will occupy most of the chapter, this passage is full of deft little touches which invite us to enter into the scene imaginatively and, perhaps, identify with one or other of the characters.

The exchange between Jesus, Philip and Andrew – and the unnamed boy with the bread and fish – is told far more intimately than in the other gospels. Indeed, Philip and Andrew are not given speaking parts at all in the other gospels; John has retained a sense of their different personalities and roles, as he has with some of the others, notably (as we shall see later) Thomas. Philip and Andrew occur again in this kind of way in 12.22; it's as though they were the **disciples** most likely to be in touch with, and establishing friendly relations with, the people around the circle of the **Twelve**. Here it's Andrew who has got to know the boy with the food, and who introduces him to Jesus.

Philip doesn't know what to do. Andrew doesn't either, but he brings the boy and his bread and fish to Jesus' attention. The point is obvious, but we perhaps need to be reminded of it: so often we ourselves have no idea what to do, but the starting point is always to bring what is there to the attention of Jesus. You can never tell what he's going to do with it – though part of Christian **faith** is the expectation that he will do something we hadn't thought of, something new and creative.

The reaction of the people – and the response of Jesus to their reaction – are both very telling. Remember how **John the Baptist** emphatically declared that he was not the **Messiah**, and nor was he 'the prophet' (1.20–21)? Here, in verse 14, we have 'the prophet' spoken of again: the 'prophet like Moses', predicted in Deuteronomy 18, the coming great leader who would do for the people what Moses did, leading them from slavery to freedom.

Jesus' hearers quickly make the jump from 'prophet' to 'Messiah', in other words, to 'king'. If Jesus is the great prophet promised so long ago, then he is the one to lead the people now. This is heavily ironic; because of course John believes, and wants us to believe, that Jesus is the Messiah, that he is indeed the prophet like Moses. But the reaction of the crowds shows that they understand both of these in what Jesus regards as a quite inadequate sense. In much of the rest of the chapter, Jesus will attempt to move them towards a deeper and truer understanding. We must hope and pray that this chapter has that effect on us as well.

JOHN 6.16–25

Jesus Walking on the Water

[16]When it was evening, Jesus' disciples went down to the seashore. [17]They got into a boat, and went across the sea towards Capernaum. It was already getting dark, and Jesus had not yet come to them. [18]A strong wind blew up, and the sea began to get rough. [19]They had been rowing for about three or four miles when they saw Jesus walking on the sea, coming towards the boat. They were terrified.

[20]But he spoke to them.

'It's me!' he said. 'Don't be afraid!'

[21]Then they were eager to take him into the boat; and at once the boat arrived at the land they had been making for.

[22]The next day the crowd that had remained on the far side of the lake saw that there had only been the one boat there. They knew that Jesus hadn't gone with his disciples, but that the disciples had set off by themselves. [23]But other boats came from Tiberias, near the place where they had eaten the bread after the Lord had given thanks. [24]When the crowd saw that neither Jesus nor his disciples were there, they themselves got into the boats and came to Capernaum looking for Jesus.

[25]When they found him beside the sea, they said to him, 'Rabbi, when did you get here?'

Some animals are naturally afraid of water. Cats will not normally go for a swim in a river; nor will hedgehogs. Most monkeys and apes, despite sharing some other characteristics of humans, do not care for water. This fact is exploited at a key moment in the movie *Planet of the Apes*, when a small group of humans fleeing from an army of apes swim across a small lake, leaving their pursuers frustrated in the rear.

That scene, like much else in the movie, is of course an echo of a biblical story, and there are no surprises here in discovering which one it is. John has already made it clear that this chapter is to be all about the **Exodus**, and so when we have this scene of Jesus walking on the water we should be prepared to understand it as part of the same story. The children of Israel began their journey to freedom by coming through the Red Sea, with the waters parting before them but closing again on their pursuers. It was, of course, Moses who led the way through the Red Sea, and the crowds have just declared that Jesus is 'the prophet who should come into the world' – the prophet, that is, like Moses (verse 14; see Deuteronomy 18.15). Now, even though the crowds have misunderstood what such a prophet might have come to do – they were looking for another act of political liberation, but Jesus was offering something far greater and deeper – Jesus nevertheless does something which the **disciples**, in subsequent reflection, are bound to see in terms of the Exodus story, the Passover story.

They would see it like this not least because the Jewish people were not keen on the sea. They were not much of a seafaring race, unlike the ancient Phoenicians to the north. In some of their ancient stories, the sea was associated with chaos, evil, untameable forces within the natural or the spiritual world. True, they sang psalms which celebrated the fact that YHWH, their God, was king over the mighty waters (e.g. Psalm 93.3–4). But even the fishermen, used to squalls on the Sea of Galilee, could find themselves not only in trouble but in fear of their lives, as the sea would suddenly become rough, and chaos threatened to come again.

All of this is in John's mind as he tells of how Jesus carried on praying on the mountain, away from the excited crowds, until late in the evening, while the disciples set off back to Capernaum in the boat. The lake is about twelve miles long by seven wide at its widest point, and it looks as though they had rowed, through the storm, most of the way back from the east side of the lake to Capernaum on the north side, when Jesus came to them walking on the water.

This event is recorded by Matthew and Mark as well as by John – with all three of them locating it immediately after the feeding of the multitude – and there is no way of rationalizing it (people used to suggest that maybe Jesus was standing on a sandbank near the shore, or something equally banal). You either come to the text with a view of what is and isn't possible in the world, which won't allow any fresh evidence – which is not, perhaps, the best way of approaching a book like John, which is all about the challenge of the **gospel** to all existing world-views – or you come with at least an open mind to new possibilities hitherto unimagined.

This isn't the same as being gullible, or credulous. Nor are the extraordinary stories in the gospels designed, as some seem to have imagined, to portray Jesus as being able to do anything at all, simply for the sake of making a supernatural display. They are there, rather, as moments in the text when the strange glory of the **Word**-made-flesh shines through, not so much because Jesus can do whatever he wants but because this particular thing is so closely associated with what Israel's God does at a key moment in Israel's history.

The reaction of the crowd is explained in detail by John. He wants to rub our noses in the fact not only that the disciples saw what had happened but also that the crowds were puzzled. They knew Jesus hadn't set off on the boat, and yet when they managed to get to the other side of the lake they found he'd already arrived in Capernaum. It would have been difficult to make the journey by land in that time, round the north-east side of the lake. As so often, John leaves us with their puzzled question, to which Jesus will now give what seems an even more puzzling answer.

The story of Jesus' walking on the water can easily be used as a theme for meditation. There are many times in our lives – and we never know when they will strike – when, metaphorically speaking, suddenly the wind gets up and the sea becomes rough. As we struggle to make our way through, sometimes we are aware of a presence with us, which may initially be more disturbing than comforting. ('We're already nearly drowning, and now we've got ghosts following us!') But if we listen, through the roar of the waves and the wind, we may hear the voice that says, 'It's me – don't be afraid.' And if we are ready then to take Jesus on board, we may find ourselves, sooner than we expected, at the harbour where we will be calm and secure once more.

JOHN 6.26–35

Bread from Heaven

²⁶This was Jesus' reply.

'I'm telling you the solemn truth,' he said. 'You aren't looking for me because you saw signs, but because you ate as much bread as you could. ²⁷You shouldn't be working for perishable food, but for food that will last to the life of God's coming age – the food which the son of man will give you, the person whom God the father has stamped with the seal of his approval.'

²⁸'What should we be doing,' they asked him, 'so that we can be doing the work God wants?'

²⁹'This is the work God wants of you,' replied Jesus, 'that you believe in the one he sent.'

³⁰'Well, then,' they said to him, 'what sign are you going to do, so that we can see it and believe you? What work are *you* doing? ³¹Our ancestors ate the manna in the wilderness; it says in the Bible that "he gave them bread from heaven to eat".'

³²'I'm telling you the solemn truth,' Jesus replied. 'It wasn't Moses who gave you the bread from heaven. It was my father who gave you

the true bread from heaven. ³³God's bread, you see, is the one who comes down from heaven and gives life to the world.'

³⁴'Master,' they said, 'give us this bread – give it to us always!'

³⁵'I am the bread of life,' replied Jesus. 'Anyone who comes to me will never be hungry! Anyone who believes in me will never be thirsty!'

The historian was in a hurry to finish his Ph.D. There was one chapter to go, which concerned the paintings that had been so important during his period, and the influence the artists had had on the wider thought and culture of the time.

He went hastily from gallery to gallery. In every room he walked around beside the walls, scribbling in his notebook, taking down all the details from the printed notices underneath the paintings. He wrote down the artists' names, their dates, where they lived, the names of their key paintings, who their friends were, what influence others had had on them, and they on others. As soon as he was finished he went on to the next gallery.

He finished his Ph.D. But at no time, in all the art galleries, had he ever stood back and looked at the paintings themselves, and allowed them to speak in their own language.

Jesus is clearly anxious that the people whom he had fed with the loaves and fishes are going to end up like that unfortunate historian. The printed notes were there to lead the eye, the mind and the heart to appreciate the paintings, not so that they could be used in a purely mechanical fashion of processing information. The bread and the fish that Jesus had distributed to the crowds were there to lead the eye, the mind and the heart to the true gift of God to his people, then and there. They were there to open up their understanding to the fact that the new Passover, the new **Exodus**, was taking place right in front of them, and that Jesus was leading it.

At first sight Jesus' warning seems almost churlish. He has done something remarkable; they are excited and come to him wanting more; and he all but rebukes them for having the wrong motivation. What else could you expect from them? But underneath the warning of verses 26 and 27 is his recognition that after the feeding in the wilderness they were only a moment away from making him king (verse 15) – and they would have meant him to be a king like other kings, a strong this-worldly figure who would lead them in their strong this-worldly agendas. Jesus is indeed a king, but the type and manner of his kingship will be very different from what the crowds expected or wanted, as we shall see in chapter 19 in particular.

Here his charge against the crowds is that the 'sign' of the feeding (are you still counting the 'signs'?) is meant to lead you to the true food:

the food the **son of man** will give (verse 27), the food which *is* Jesus himself (verse 35). What matters is not just what Jesus can do for you; what matters is who Jesus *is*. Only if you're prepared to be confronted by that in a new way can you begin to understand what he can really do for you, what he really wants to do for you. Only if the eager note-taker is prepared to stop and ask what these signs are *for* can he ever pause, lift his eyes and enter into the actual world of the artist instead of remaining in the world of the hurried would-be scholar.

The question of who Jesus really is now comes to the fore, and will steadily dominate the discussion both in this chapter and in those to come. First, he is the one upon whom the father has set his seal (verse 27): God, like a goldsmith with a hallmark, or like a king with his great seal, has stamped this person with the mark that declares not only where he comes from but that he carries his authority. What Jesus is doing, in other words, bears the marks that say: this is the kind of thing that, in Israel's scriptures, God himself does. The wilderness feeding and the walking on water speak of this in ways that, though quite different, are both related to the Exodus story.

Second, the demand that God is making on them – the crowd realize that Jesus is pointing out that they can't just expect bread on demand, that if this really is a **heaven**-sent renewal movement there will be a new standard to which they must sign up. This means that God is making a demand on them, and it is this: that they believe in Jesus. No new exposition of the detailed commandments of the **law**; rather, a command which, if it is to be obeyed, will require a change of heart.

It will require, in particular, the recognition that in Jesus, and in everything he is doing, the same God is at work who was at work in the Exodus story. It seems odd that they ask for a further sign, when Jesus has just given them one. Perhaps they were hoping for something more obviously military and political. Perhaps they wanted Jesus to march on Jerusalem and make the walls fall down, as Joshua had done with Jericho at the conclusion of the Exodus. Jesus doesn't answer their request for a further sign, but instead points out that the real answer to their question is standing in front of them. Moses was only God's agent. What was going on, all along, was that God was providing not just the physical bread dropping down from the sky (Exodus 16), but the spiritual nourishment which kept alive their **faith** and hope. That was what God was doing then, and that was what he was doing now.

The passage ends, climactically, with the first of the famous 'I am' sayings in John's **gospel** (verse 35). (This one is so important that it's repeated twice, in verses 48 and 51.) It looks on to others, such as 8.12 ('I am the light of the world'), which we shall examine in due course. And of course it is another way of saying what the Prologue said: Jesus is the **Word**, the one who comes from the father into the world to accomplish his purpose. And in this case the particular emphasis is on nourishment. Until they recognize who Jesus really is, they may be fed with bread and fish, but there is a deep hunger inside them which will never be satisfied. Verse 34 can be used to this day, as it stands, as the prayer that we all need to pray if our deepest needs are to be met.

JOHN 6.36–46

The Father's Will

[36]'But I told you', Jesus continued, 'that you have indeed seen me – and still you don't believe! [37]All that the father gives me will come to me; and I won't reject anyone who comes to me, [38]because I came down from heaven not to do my own will but the will of the one who sent me. [39]And this is the will of the one who sent me, that I should lose nothing out of everything that he has given me, but that I should raise it up on the last day. [40]This is the will of my father, you see: that all who see the son and believe in him should have the life of God's coming age; and I will raise them up on the last day.'

[41]The Judaeans then grumbled about him because he had said, 'I am the bread which came down from heaven.'

[42]'Isn't this Jesus, Joseph's son?' they said. 'We know his father and mother, don't we? So how can he say "I came down from heaven"?'

[43]'Don't grumble among yourselves,' answered Jesus. [44]'No one can come to me unless the father who sent me draws them – and I will raise them up on the last day. [45]It is written in the prophets, "They shall all be taught by God." Everyone who listens to what comes from the father, and learns from it, comes to me. [46]Not that anyone has seen the father except the one who is from God; he has seen the father.'

C. S. Lewis was once interviewed by an American Christian journalist who was writing about well-known characters who had converted to Christianity during adult life. The theme was 'decision'. He wanted to get Lewis to say how he had 'made his decision'.

Unfortunately for his project, Lewis refused to put it in those terms. He hadn't 'made a decision', he said. God had closed in on him and he couldn't escape (though at the time he had badly wanted to). The closest he would get to using the language the reporter was interested in was to say, 'I was decided upon.' In his autobiography, *Surprised by Joy*, he describes it in a more evocative phrase: 'His compulsion is our liberation.'

One of the hard lessons the children of Israel had to learn in the wilderness was that their God, YHWH, was not at their beck and call.

He wasn't obliged to them. He hadn't decided to rescue them from Egypt because they were a great nation, more powerful and numerous than others. He certainly hadn't discovered that they were a particularly moral or godly people. There was nothing in them, as they stood, to commend them to him. It was simply that in his loving choice he had decided to make them his own people, so that they would be the nation through whom his purposes and love would be made known to the world. This is particularly emphasized in Deuteronomy 7.7–11 – which is, significantly, set in the context of Moses going through the story of how much Israel had grumbled and provoked their God in the wilderness.

We shouldn't be surprised, then, that we find the same blend of themes here. The Judaeans – Jesus' regular opponents in this **gospel** – are here grumbling, like the people in the wilderness in the **Exodus** story. They are looking for the kind of leader, or **Messiah**, who will give them what they want. Jesus' rather startling emphasis on the sovereignty of Israel's God in choosing the people he is going to 'draw' to believe in Jesus has the same function as the warnings of Deuteronomy 7: don't suppose that, because you are part of God's chosen people, that must mean you are special in and of yourselves.

The 'drawing' of the father (verse 43) of those he has 'given' to the son (verse 37) takes place, it seems, in the silent secret places of the human heart. When Jesus quotes 'they shall all be taught by God' from Isaiah 54.13, he is calling to mind one of the Old Testament's greatest prophecies of the renewal that will come about through the great outpouring of God's love, bringing his people back from **exile**. The passage goes on, soon afterwards (Isaiah 55.1), to invite everyone who is thirsty to come to the waters and drink freely – picking up what Jesus has just said in verse 35 ('the one who believes in me shall never be thirsty'). Jesus seems to have the whole passage in mind.

Part of the point of the Isaiah passage is the complete helplessness of Israel at the time. That's why God must take the initiative, as here. That is why, too, the exclusive claim is made that only 'the one sent from God' has actually seen God (verse 46). Only when people are humble enough to recognize God's unique revelation in and to Jesus can they then taste the bread from **heaven**. But God's initiative is always balanced, in the Bible, with an open and free appeal: anyone at all who is thirsty is invited to come to the water that is on offer; anyone at all who comes to Jesus will not be rejected.

This passage introduces, for the second time in this gospel, the promise which goes beyond 'eternal life', which could otherwise be a vague and imprecise 'life after death'. Those who come to Jesus in **faith** are promised that he will raise them up on the last day (verses

59

39, 40, 44). This helps to explain the hope that is on offer throughout John's gospel.

'Eternal life' is the quality of life, sharing the inner life of Jesus, that is on offer at once to anyone who believes. 'Eternal' tells you what *sort* of life it is, as well as the fact that it goes on after death: it is the life of the **age to come**, the new life which God has always planned to give to his world. But the form that this eternal life will take in the end is not that of the disembodied spirit that so many people today assume is what Christians think about life after death. The eternal life that begins in the present when someone believes, and continues in the future beyond death, will eventually take the form of the **resurrection** life already spoken of in 5.25–29. The entire story John is telling is designed to end with Jesus pioneering the way into this newly embodied life, and the promise of the present chapter is that this life will be shared by all who taste of the living bread.

JOHN 6.47–59

Eating and Drinking the Son of Man

[47]'I'm telling you the solemn truth,' Jesus went on. 'Anyone who believes in me has the life of God's coming age. [48]I am the bread of life. [49]Your ancestors in the wilderness ate the manna, and they died. [50]This is the bread which comes down from heaven, so that people can eat it and not die. [51]I am the living bread which came down from heaven. If anyone eats from this bread, they will live for ever. And the bread which I shall give is my flesh, given for the life of the world.'

[52]This caused a squabble among the Judaeans.

'How can this fellow give us his flesh to eat?' they asked.

[53]'I'm telling you the solemn truth,' Jesus replied. 'If you don't eat the flesh of the son of man, and drink his blood, you have no life in yourselves. [54]Anyone who feasts upon my flesh and drinks my blood has the life of God's coming age, and I will raise them up on the last day. [55]My flesh is true food, you see, and my blood is true drink. [56]Anyone who eats my flesh and drinks my blood remains in me, and I remain in them. [57]Just as the living father sent me, and I live because of the father, so the one who eats me will live because of me. [58]This is the bread which came down from heaven; it isn't like the bread which the ancestors ate, and died. The one who eats this bread will share the life of God's new age.'

[59]He said this in the synagogue, while he was teaching in Capernaum.

One of the most moving, and often forgotten, stories about King David concerns the time when he was fighting the Philistines, who had

60

occupied his native town of Bethlehem. Among David's fiercely loyal fighting men he had three in particular who were renowned for their bravery and their readiness to do whatever the king might ask. When he and his men were pinned down one day, David longed for a drink, and said out loud how much he would like to have water from the well at Bethlehem – which was of course inaccessible due to the Philistines. But that didn't stop his three heroes. Off they went, broke through the Philistine army, got water from the well at Bethlehem and brought it back to David.

But David didn't drink it. His shrewd sense of political judgment was even sharper than his thirst.

'God forbid', he said, 'that I should drink the blood of these men, who went at the risk of their lives' (2 Samuel 23.17; 1 Chronicles 11.19). He didn't want to be seen to profit from their readiness to put their lives on the line for him. He poured the water out on the ground.

Fancy a Jew talking about drinking blood! One of the best-known of the many Jewish regulations about food and drink was that blood was absolutely forbidden (Leviticus 17.10–14 is the central statement of the principle). Indeed, the complex system of kosher butchering has this among its chief aims, that no blood should remain in the animal and so risk being eaten or drunk. And this, of course, was why David used the phrase. To drink this water would be the equivalent of drinking blood. He wouldn't – he shouldn't – he couldn't do it.

But the fact that Jesus speaks of 'drinking his blood' in this setting gives us an all-important clue to what he means in this extraordinary passage. If you want to profit from what I'm doing, he says, you must 'eat my flesh' and 'drink my blood'. If you do this, you'll live for ever; I will raise you up on the last day. In the light of the David story, we can confidently say that the deep meaning of the passage is not that those who believe in him should become cannibals, still less that they should, in 'eating' and 'drinking' him, break the Jewish **law** against consuming blood. What he means is what David meant. He refused to 'drink the blood' of his comrades – that is, to profit from the risk of their lives. Jesus, as the true **Messiah**, is going one better again. *He* will put his own life at risk – indeed, he will actually lose it; and *his* comrades will profit from that death. They will 'drink his blood'. They will have their thirst quenched by his death and all that it means.

Now of course it would be possible to 'spiritualize' the language of eating and drinking so that it only meant an inner, non-physical event, of meditation, celebration and grateful contemplation. All of these are important, but John insists here, as does Paul in 1 Corinthians 10 and 11, that the 'eating' and 'drinking' in question must include actual physical eating and drinking. Indeed, in verses 54–58 the word for 'eat' is a very solidly physical one. It was often used by Greek speakers to mean something like 'munch' or 'chew', and might be used of the way that animals ate, making a noise as they did so. It may well be that some in the early church, remembering Jesus' words most likely in the original Aramaic language that he spoke, were tempted (quite understandably) to spiritualize their meaning, and to lose any sense that he really meant to refer to an actual feeding; and John, in writing in Greek, deliberately chooses a word which rules this out.

Easily the best explanation for this – though one which has proved controversial in recent centuries – is that John understands Jesus' language here to refer to the **eucharist**, the Lord's supper, the sacrament in which Jesus' body and blood are, in a mysterious way, offered to believers to be eaten and drunk.

John does not describe the actual meal at the Last Supper, just as he doesn't describe the actual **baptism** of Jesus. But this, we may suppose, is not because he thinks it doesn't matter, or that he wants to play it down, but because he thinks it matters so much that it's important to see it as affecting the whole **gospel** story. So here, after the feeding in the wilderness, where (as in the other gospels) Jesus' action with the bread is described in words very like those used at the Supper itself (verse 11), we find a long discourse in which, here at its climax, Jesus declares that in order for him to be truly united with his believing followers, it is necessary for them to 'munch' his flesh and drink his blood.

Those who do this will be people of the true **Exodus**. In the original Exodus, the ancestors of the present Israelites had eaten the bread they were given, but they still died. This bread, this bread-of-life which is Jesus himself, is given, and given to be broken in death, so that those who eat of it may not die, but experience **the life of God's coming age** in the present and the future and be raised up on the last day.

It won't come as a surprise that this caused a fuss (verse 52). It still does today. But what we might call 'sacramental' thinking is absolutely central to John's gospel. If the **Word** has become flesh (1.14), we shouldn't be surprised if the same principle is designed by God to work its way through the whole creation.

There is a very careful balance to be kept, as the next passage will make clear. We can't imagine that the whole creation is now 'sacramental' in this sense, as though there were nothing now wrong with any of it, and as though any experience of the created order were somehow pregnant with the presence of Jesus. That way leads straight to pantheism, nature mysticism and idolatry.

Nor can we suppose that anyone who takes the Christian sacrament carelessly and without real **faith** is somehow to be 'magically' saved for ever. God isn't fooled. Eating and drinking is no good without faith, without the **spirit** (see verses 63–64).

But it remains true that 'God so loved the world' (3.16), and that the world he loved, having once contained the Word made Flesh, is now waiting, like a beautiful crystal glass waiting to be filled with rich wine, for the day when God will flood it completely with his own presence (see Romans 8.18–25). John, like some other early Christian writers, was prepared to see the bread and wine of the eucharist as foretastes of that great moment. Certainly almost all his first readers will have read verses 53–58 in this way. At this point to understand the text more fully requires that we do something: the thing which Jesus himself commanded 'in remembrance of me' (Luke 22.19; 1 Corinthians 11.25).

JOHN 6.60–71

Division among Jesus' Followers

[60]When they heard this, many of Jesus' disciples said, 'This is difficult stuff! Who can bear to listen to it?'

[61]Jesus knew in himself that his disciples were grumbling about what he'd said.

'Does this put you off?' he said. [62]'What if you were to see the son of man ascending to where he was before? [63]It's the spirit that gives life; the flesh is no help. The words that I have spoken to you – they are spirit, they are life. [64]But there are some of you who don't believe.'

Jesus knew from the beginning, you see, those who didn't believe, and the one who was going to betray him.

[65]'That's why I said', he went on, 'that no one can come to me unless it is given to them by the father.'

[66]From that time on, several of his disciples drew back, and no longer went about with him.

[67]Jesus turned to the Twelve.

'You don't want to go away too, do you?' he asked.

[68]Simon Peter spoke up.

'Master', he said, 'who can we go to? You're the one who's got the life-giving words of the age to come! [69]We've come to believe it – we've come to know it! – that you are God's holy one.'

[70]'Well', replied Jesus, 'I chose you twelve, didn't I? And one of you is an accuser!'

[71]He was referring to Judas, son of Simon Iscariot. He was one of the Twelve, and he was going to betray him.

I once went to a lecture that was supposed to be an introduction to philosophy. It quickly appeared that the great philosopher wasn't interested in introducing the subject, but in talking about it at a high level to the small group of eager postgraduates who already knew the basics and wanted to go further. I didn't go back.

That was not, I think, the problem in verse 60. It wasn't that Jesus was talking at too abstract a level – though no doubt there were some who found their heads spinning after the long discussion in the Capernaum synagogue. It was more that what he had said made a huge hole in their world-view, and when that happens some people prefer not to think about it any more. If you go to a meeting where someone demolishes the way you've been brought up to think, and offers you instead a way of looking at the world which, though convincing, will be extremely costly, you may well find good reasons to be somewhere else next time the preacher comes to town.

Several of his hearers, then, continue to grumble – continuing the theme of the Israelites grumbling in the wilderness, even while the **Exodus** was proceeding, and God was feeding them with the manna. This new teaching was 'difficult' in the sense that it was demanding not just to get your mind round it but to get your heart and soul into it. For anyone brought up in one of the varieties of first-century Judaism, all that Jesus had said was demanding in every sense, but most particularly in that, whereas they might have been prepared to follow a prophet like Moses, or a would-be **Messiah**, as long as such figures kept within the bounds of the agendas and aspirations they had had in mind, the thought of someone who would speak as Jesus had spoken was too much.

There was therefore a division among his followers. It looks as though the majority refused to go with him any longer, with only **the Twelve** continuing. This is bound to be an oversimplification; clearly, when Jesus arrives in Jerusalem in chapter 12, there is a large crowd with him, and many who did not completely understand, but who were not repelled either, will have continued. But the effect of chapter 6 persists.

Indeed, it could be said that chapter 6, with its striking claims from Jesus, and its extraordinary language about eating his flesh and drinking his blood, remains to this day the cause of a different, though perhaps related, division: between those who think that John's **gospel** is simply incredible as a historical record of things Jesus did and said, and those who are prepared to hold open their minds to the possibility that Jesus, in addition to teaching in the way described in Matthew, Mark and Luke, might also have given this sort of in-depth and challenging teaching to his followers. That debate continues, and I don't want to go further into it, except to say this.

I notice that a prejudice against taking John historically seems to go very closely with moves within Western culture to think of religion as a purely spiritual thing. It doesn't matter, we're told, if these things happened or not, whether they were said or not; what matters is the spiritual truth that they are teaching. That sounds fine (a bit too fine, actually); but it can't be what John was meaning. This whole discourse, and indeed the whole gospel, are about the **Word** becoming flesh: not the Word becoming an idea, a spirituality, a feeling, or an experience. John may be writing something like history or he may not; but part of what he is trying to tell us is that history – the actual story of Jesus – matters.

At the same time (this is the point of verses 62 and 63, which are the heart of this passage), the explanation for how the whole thing fits together is given by mentioning two things: the ascension of Jesus, and the **spirit**. At first sight this seems only to confuse an already complicated set of problems still further. But these are the keys to unlock the puzzles.

The mention of the ascension of the **son of man** (as in 3.13) is designed to say: maybe you need to come to terms with the fact that the one you are now dealing with is equally at home in **heaven** and on earth. He is a citizen of both. He is, after all, the Word made flesh. If that is so, it makes sense to suppose that this flesh, and this blood, are somehow vehicles of the inner life of the Word. The flesh by itself, of course, would be irrelevant, as verse 63 says. But when the flesh is indwelt by the life of God, of the Word who is God, it makes sense to speak of it in the way Jesus has just done. Though the ascension as an event remains mysterious in John's gospel (Jesus speaks of it in 20.17, but it is not described), it is clearly important for John, here and elsewhere, to affirm that Jesus' body, not just his 'spiritual' life, was and remains the place where the Word took up permanent residence.

Jesus will have more to say about the spirit as the gospel progresses. Here he is warning against a purely physical interpretation of his words about eating and drinking. He is urging his hearers, as he has been doing all along, to go beyond a one-dimensional understanding of what he is doing and saying (for instance, a desire to follow him to get more free bread) and to break through to listen to the Word within the flesh. For this, they will need the spirit to help them. Without that, they will remain in unbelief.

The Twelve, however, remain. They are prepared to say out loud that Jesus is God's holy one, his Messiah. He is the one who is not only speaking *about* God's new age, the **age to come**, but is, by his words, already bringing it into existence: 'You're the one who's got the life-giving words of the age to come.' Jesus knows that one of them will turn traitor, and, worse than traitor, become an 'accuser' (the word can mean '**devil**', but here and elsewhere John seems to refer to what Judas was actually going to do in handing Jesus over to the courts). But for the moment the Twelve stand as representatives of the **faith**, the belief, that Jesus has been looking for: the recognition that in him, his words and his deeds, Israel's God was at last bringing into being the new Exodus, the great movement that would set the whole world free from sin and death.

JOHN 7.1–9

Jesus and His Brothers

[1]After this, Jesus went about in Galilee. He didn't want to go about in Judaea, because the Judaeans were after his blood.

[2]The time came for the Jewish festival of Tabernacles. [3]So Jesus' brothers approached him.

'Leave this place', they said, 'and go to Judaea! Then your disciples will see the works you're doing. [4]Nobody who wants to become well known does things in secret. If you're doing these things, show yourself to the world!'

[5]Even his brothers, you see, didn't believe in him.

[6]'My time isn't here yet', replied Jesus, 'but your time is always here. [7]The world can't hate you, but it hates me, because I am giving evidence against it, showing that its works are evil. [8]I tell you what: you go up to the feast. I'm not going up to this feast; my time is not yet complete.'

[9]With these words, he stayed behind in Galilee.

Many Jewish communities around the world keep the festival of Tabernacles, or 'Booths', to this day. The 'tabernacles' in question are usually makeshift shelters, made out of whatever comes to hand, set up in the open air in a back yard or porch. They may be used for meals, or even for sleeping. Their purpose, like so many Jewish traditions, is to remind the people of the time when their ancestors wandered in the wilderness, living in tents, that is, 'tabernacles' or 'booths'.

It was also an agricultural festival, coming at the climax of the harvest season, celebrating the harvest of grapes and olives in particular. In the time of Jesus it was one of the three great annual pilgrimage feasts (the others being Passover and Pentecost), when tens of thousands of Jewish people would converge on Jerusalem. All kinds of lavish celebrations took place, involving lighting of lamps, dancing by torchlight, processions that ended with the pouring out of water and wine in the **Temple**, and a march of **priests** and people around the altar carrying citrus fruit and waving palm branches. The festival, like Passover, was regarded as a key symbol of the great national hope: the coming of the **Messiah**, and liberation from Rome. The celebrations went on for a full eight days, starting and ending with a special **sabbath**.

John is the only **gospel** that mentions a celebration of this festival, and the chapter begins here with all kinds of teasing hints of what is to come. Will Jesus go up to Jerusalem for the festival, or won't he? What does he mean by talking of his 'time', which isn't here yet? What are his brothers trying to get him to do?

Let's begin with the last of these. Jesus' brothers (who, again, play more of a role in John than in the other gospels) seem to be half believing and half not. They see that he's doing remarkable things, but they don't 'believe' in the full sense that John is talking about. They see Jesus simply as an extraordinary wonder-worker who might well gain a larger following if only he would appear on a larger stage: Galilee wasn't exactly a backwater, but Jerusalem was where everything happened that seemed to matter. But they have no sense that his mission will involve a single, final, decisive action through which Israel and the world will be changed for good.

That is the main difference in this passage between Jesus and them. Jesus is aware of a 'time' which is coming – but which hasn't come yet. Like a skilled sailor watching for the moment when the tide begins to turn, then waiting for the moment when it will be full enough to set sail, he has a plan in mind which will gradually come to light. And the plan, as John has already been hinting to us, has a Passover shape to it, not a Tabernacles shape. As we shall see later in the chapter, there are things about the festival of Booths which Jesus regards as pointing forwards to his own achievement. But Passover is when the lamb will be sacrificed.

Jesus' 'time', then, will not come this autumn, but – so John is hinting – in the spring. It wouldn't be right, then, for him to go to Jerusalem in the pilgrim convoy, healing and teaching as he went, gathering more followers en route and building up expectations of a great moment of deliverance, suggesting that Jesus was now to be declared as Messiah. As we shall see in the next passage, Jesus follows his brothers up to the festival, but does so quietly and without show. He is biding his time – and John, telling us that, is keeping us in suspense to see what that time will bring when it finally arrives.

The contrast between Jesus and his brothers is expressed in verse 7 in terms of the attitudes of 'the world'. We learn in verse 1 that the Judaeans (i.e., the inhabitants of the area around Jerusalem, as opposed to the Galileans in the north) were looking for a chance to kill Jesus, as they had been since at least his previous visit (5.18). This will be a major theme of the present chapter, where Jesus accuses them of plotting against him (verses 19 and 25), and where indeed his actions and teaching prompt plans to arrest him. And when Jesus says that 'the world' hates him, this is what he seems to be referring to.

This explains, at least in part, what John means by 'the world'. At one level, it means the whole created universe, including all the peoples of the earth. But at another level it means the deep-seated attitude that turns away from the loving creator, and tries to organize its life independently of him. The problem which gives this gospel its particular flavour is this: Jerusalem, and its leaders and opinion-formers both official and unofficial, has come to embody the attitudes of 'the world'. When Jesus goes to Jerusalem he is, indeed, 'showing himself to the world', but it is a world turned against the God it continues outwardly to celebrate, a world that doesn't want to know of his strange, loving purposes.

But those loving purposes themselves are, in fact, advanced by this. God chose Israel to be his representative people, the light of the world. If Israel, in the persons of the national leaders, has turned away from this vocation, that doesn't stop them still standing in a special position between God and the world. It is as though, now, the sorrow and anger, the evil and rebellion, of all the world has been concentrated in Jerusalem, so that when Jesus goes to Jerusalem he is facing not only a local and national problem but the problem of the whole world, the world that God loved so much (3.16). The world, of course, doesn't enjoy being told that it's radically out of line (verse 7); but it cannot at the moment see that the doctor who is diagnosing the disease is also about to provide the remedy.

JOHN 7.10–18

Disputes about Jesus

[10]But when Jesus' brothers had gone up to the festival, then he himself went up, not openly, but, so to speak, in secret. [11]The Judaeans were looking for him at the feast.

'Where is he?' they were saying.

[12]There was considerable dispute about him among the crowds.

'He's a good man!' some were saying.

'No, he isn't,' others would reply. 'He's deceiving the people!'

[13]But nobody dared speak about him openly, for fear of the Judaeans.

[14]About the middle of the feast, Jesus went up into the Temple and began to teach. [15]The Judaeans were astonished.

'Where does this fellow get all his learning from?' they asked. 'He's never been trained!'

[16]'My teaching isn't my own,' replied Jesus. 'It comes from the one who sent me! [17]If anyone wants to do what God wants, they will know whether this teaching is from God, or whether I'm just speaking on

my own account. [18]Anyone who speaks on his own behalf is trying to establish his own reputation. But if what he's interested in is the reputation of the one who sent him, then he is true, and there is no injustice in him.'

'You'll find out how when you really want to.'

Jeff's mother was trying, not for the first time, to teach him how to cook. He just couldn't get the hang of it. He would see what she was doing and copy her, but when he tried later to do it himself he would do things in the wrong order, forget vital ingredients, or leave things burning on the stove. His heart just wasn't in it.

'Well,' repeated his mother, 'one of these days you'll have to do it for yourself, and then you'll learn soon enough.'

The same is true in several areas of life. The teenage girl who hates learning a foreign language suddenly becomes keen on it when, on holiday abroad, she meets an attractive young man who doesn't speak much of her language. The young man who's never bothered to learn to swim suddenly wants to do so when all his friends are going sailing and tell him he must learn to swim if he's going to feel safe in the boat.

As so often, these illustrations point towards what Jesus is saying without exhausting its significance. The central clue to this passage is verse 17: if anyone wants to do God's will, they will know whether the teaching which Jesus is giving comes from God, or whether he's just making it up to boost his own position and reputation. If, that is, somebody really intends to do God's will when they discover it, then it will become clear to them that Jesus really is from God.

The trouble is, of course, that the Judaeans, perhaps not surprisingly, are coming at it the other way round. First they want to weigh up Jesus' teaching, and then they'll decide whether he's been sent by God or not. That would be all very well if they were, so to speak, neutral observers; but there is no neutrality when you're faced with prophecy, or national crises, or huge challenges to an entire way of life. In their weighing up of Jesus, many of them have settled it in their minds that there are certain things which they do *not* want God to be saying to them; and if Jesus says those things, then they will rule him out of consideration right away.

The controversy about what they should make of Jesus comes to boiling point in this passage, and will continue that way more or less right through now to chapter 12. The two options are stated quite starkly in verse 12. Some people approve of him, but others suggest he is a deceiver.

That charge is worse than it might sound. As far back as Deuteronomy 13 there were biblical warnings that false prophets and teachers would arise within Israel, performing signs and wonders in order to lead Israel astray to worship foreign gods, to turn aside from the path marked out by YHWH. The penalty for such behaviour was clear: someone deceiving the people in this way was to be put to death. And several of the Judaeans thought that when Jesus told the cripple to carry his mattress on the **sabbath**, as recorded in chapter 5, that was the telltale sign that he was in fact leading Israel away from the **law**, and hence from God.

The other question to which Jesus is responding concerns the source of his teaching. Teachers in Judaism would normally have studied the law with one or more **rabbis**. They would have spent years perfecting their knowledge of the finer points of interpretation. Jesus had never attended such classes, and yet he obviously knew the scriptures extremely well and was able to expound them in a fresh and vivid way. Where had he got it all from?

The two issues come together into the question: is Jesus from God, or is he acting on his own authority? This is the question to which verses 16–18 are the answer. In verse 16 Jesus states his response baldly: his teaching comes from God, and he didn't make it up himself. Verse 17 then expands this with a challenge: maybe the reason you can't see it comes from God is that you've already closed your mind against what God really wants from you. Maybe, like the young person who's not motivated to learn a new skill, you need to come to the position where you really want God's will, whatever it may mean for you, whatever it will cost. If you get to that position, then what Jesus is saying will be like a cool, fresh drink on a hot and sultry afternoon. You will know, deep within yourself, that he and his teaching are from God. This challenge was powerful in Jesus' own day and remains powerful today.

Verse 18 sets the whole matter within a larger picture. Whose reputation is Jesus building up? His own, or God's? His brothers, as we saw earlier, were keen that he should build up his own reputation. They wanted him to appear in public as often as possible and become as well known as he could. Jesus was not only working to a different timetable (verse 8), but to a different programme. He was not trying to boost his own reputation, but God's. Otherwise, why would he do things that would get him into trouble, and provoke threats on his life? The ultimate answer to the question comes when Jesus goes to his death, out of obedient love for God and self-giving love for his people (13.1). People who are seeking their own repute would not act in that way.

This remains the answer, today, to those who challenge Christians on the truth of their **message**. Are we speaking the truth, or are we only doing it to boost our own status, prestige or wealth? Many times in the history of the church people have accused preachers and teachers of the latter, and sometimes they have been proved right. Verse 17 is important here, too: people often accuse Christians of advancing their own ideas rather than God's when the people concerned don't really want to hear what God has to say to them. Blaming the church is a convenient way of ignoring God's costly and demanding call. But verse 18 still forms as much a challenge to today's church as to today's world. If the church is really living out the sacrificial love of Jesus, for God and the world, it will become clear that it is not seeking its own glory, but the glory of the one who has called and sent it.

JOHN 7.19–30

Moses and the Messiah

¹⁹'Moses gave you the law, didn't he?' Jesus continued. 'But none of you obeys the law. Why are you wanting to kill me?'

²⁰The crowd responded to this.

'You must have a demon inside you!' they said. 'Who is trying to kill you?'

²¹'Look here,' replied Jesus. 'I did one single thing, and you are all amazed. ²²Moses commanded you to practise circumcision (not that it starts with Moses, of course; it comes from the patriarchs), and you circumcise a man on the sabbath. ²³Well, then, if a man receives circumcision on the sabbath, so that the law of Moses may not be broken, how can you be angry with me if I make an entire man healthy on the sabbath? ²⁴Don't judge by appearances! Judge with proper and right judgment!'

²⁵Some Jerusalem residents commented, 'Isn't this the man they're trying to kill? ²⁶Look – he's speaking quite openly, and nobody is saying anything to him. You don't suppose our rulers really know he's the Messiah, do you? ²⁷The thing is, we know where he comes from – but when the Messiah appears, nobody will know where he comes from.'

²⁸As Jesus was teaching in the Temple, he shouted out, 'You know me! You know where I come from! I haven't come on my own behalf – but the one who sent me is true, and you don't know him! ²⁹I know him, because I come from him, and he sent me!'

³⁰So they tried to arrest him. But nobody laid hands on him, because his time had not yet come.

My friend was walking with his son through a park in a Canadian city. It was a lovely summer day. The son had recently taken up golf, and was itching to practise some shots with a club he'd brought with him.

'You can't do that,' said my friend. 'There's a law against playing golf in this park.'

71

'That's a stupid law!' said the son.

'No, it's not,' responded the father. 'It's a good law. Look at all these people here. They're enjoying the park. They're having a good time. If there were people spraying golf balls all over the place, nobody would be able to relax. That's why you have golf courses, so you can play in peace and not disturb people.'

We often feel that laws are made to restrict us, to stop us doing the things we like doing. Traffic laws stop us driving as fast as we'd like to. Taxation laws make us give money to the government. And city by-laws forbid you to practise golf in a park where people are relaxing and enjoying themselves. It can seem very frustrating.

But of course all these laws are made to protect people and to enable ordinary life to go on. If everyone drove too fast, there would be more accidents, people would get hurt and the roads would get blocked with crashed cars. If nobody paid their taxes, public services would cease to operate. If everybody did what they liked in a public park, nobody would enjoy it at all.

Jesus is highlighting two radically different attitudes to the **law** of Moses. He is still referring to what had happened in chapter 5, when he healed the cripple at the pool and was then accused of **sabbath**-breaking because he told the man to carry his mattress – the charge which goes on echoing through John's **gospel**. What was the purpose of the law, he asks. Was it to stop people doing things, or to enable people to do and be what God meant them to do and be? How can something which enhances human **life** and brings dignity and hope to someone who hadn't got much of either be against the good purposes of God and his good law?

To make the point, he gives the example of **circumcision** (explaining as he does so that he knows how ancient the custom is; this kind of little detail is perhaps what the bystanders were surprised at in verse 15). In order to keep the law of Moses, he says, a boy will be circumcised on the eighth day after birth, even if it's a sabbath. In other words, something that looks as though it's breaking the sabbath has to be done even on that day, in order to make one tiny part of a baby boy's body conform to God's will. Now, supposing it's possible to make a person's entire body whole and sound on the sabbath: isn't that even more important?

Underneath all this is Jesus' regular charge against his contemporaries: that they were using certain aspects of the law to assure themselves that they really were God's people, even if in fact they broke other aspects of it (verse 19). He makes the charge all the sharper by accusing them of insisting on the sabbath law on the one hand but being ready to kill him on the other – ready to break one part of the law in order to uphold a different one. How can this be what Moses – or God, for that matter – really intended?

The reaction in Jerusalem is again mixed. Some say he has a **demon** – a charge we shall hear again, in chapters 8 and 10. Others wonder not only whether Jesus might be the **Messiah** but whether the authorities already know that he is, and so are allowing him to teach openly like this. But, in a typical misunderstanding, they declare (verse 27) that it's difficult to see him as Messiah, because they know where he comes from, whereas if he really was the Messiah that wouldn't be the case. We have other evidence that some first-century Jews believed the Messiah would appear mysteriously, with nobody knowing where he came from.

Jesus' reply is not what we expect. We imagine he's going to insist that he is the Messiah, and so to insist as well that they don't know where he has come from. But, as so often in this gospel, Jesus goes deeper than we, or his hearers, expect. He agrees that they do indeed know where he comes from – in other words, that he has come to Jerusalem from Galilee (see verses 40–52). But, instead of saying, as we might have imagined, 'But you don't know where I *really* come from', meaning from God, he turns the question round. They are indeed ignorant of something: but their real ignorance is not so much about him, Jesus, but about God. It isn't that they do know God but aren't sure if Jesus comes from God; it is, rather, that they don't even know God, and so naturally cannot associate the Jesus they are seeing with the true God.

The same challenge comes to today's world. Often people look at Jesus and draw conclusions about him based on faulty ideas of God and the world. But the Christian **message** insists that people must learn afresh who God is, what the world is, and who we ourselves are, by looking at Jesus. That is the right way round. And the challenge is often needed just as much inside the churches as outside them.

JOHN 7.31–39

Rivers of Living Water

[31]Many people from the crowd believed in Jesus.

'When the Messiah comes,' they were saying, 'will he do more signs than this man has done?'

[32]The Pharisees heard that the crowd was full of this rumour about him, and the chief priests and Pharisees sent servants to arrest him.

[33]So Jesus said, 'I'm just with you for a little while, and then I'm going to the one who sent me. [34]You will look for me and you won't find me, and you can't come where I am.'

73

³⁵'Where does he think he's going,' said the Judaeans to one another, 'if we won't be able to find him? He's not going to go off abroad, among the Greeks, is he, and teach the Greeks? ³⁶What does he mean when he says, "You'll look for me and you won't find me", and "Where I am, you can't come"?'

³⁷On the last day of the festival, the great final celebration, Jesus stood up and shouted out, 'If anybody's thirsty, they should come to me and have a drink! ³⁸Anyone who believes in me will have rivers of living water flowing out of their heart, just like the Bible says!'

³⁹He said this about the spirit, which people who believed in him were to receive. The spirit wasn't available yet, because Jesus was not yet glorified.

'A pint of water every hour, and don't forget!'

I was setting off into the desert, and my host was understandably anxious. Coming as I did from a cool and damp climate, I might easily forget how important it was to keep drinking plenty of water. Even though I was only going out for the day, to walk in the hills above the ancient settlement of **Qumran** where the **Dead Sea Scrolls** were discovered, it would be quite possible to become seriously dehydrated. Every soldier in the army, I was told, drank a pint of water every hour when they were on exercises in the desert, and so should I.

When you're in that kind of climate all sorts of things in the Bible suddenly make new sense. Most of the Bible, after all, was written in the Middle East, where much of the land is desert and water is quite simply the number-one requirement wherever you go. If a town or tribe has a good water supply, from a stream or spring or well, it can thrive; if it hasn't, it can't.

Standing in the hills above the Dead Sea, you realize in a new way where the idea came from that Jesus refers to in verse 38. You can still see the ancient aqueduct that the group at Qumran carved out of the side of the hill, so that on the rare occasions when a freak storm brought sudden 'living water' cascading down the normally dry stream beds some at least could be diverted, ending up in the large cisterns that the community had carved out as storage tanks for the long, dry weeks and months. 'Living water', as you will remember from 4.10, was the regular way of speaking of 'running water' – but of course, since 'life' is such an important theme throughout this **gospel**, we are meant to hear other echoes in the phrase as well.

But which passage in the Bible is Jesus referring to? Announcing that anyone who was thirsty could come and have a drink was obviously an echo of Isaiah 55.1, one of the great evangelistic invitations in the whole Old Testament. And John is careful to tell us that Jesus is making this invitation on the last day of the festival of Tabernacles, which as we saw in the first section of the chapter had among its celebratory rituals a moment when the **priests** would pour out water and wine around the altar. Among the prayers that were regularly prayed at the festival were prayers for rain and for the **resurrection** of the dead; so not only the theme of water, but also of new life, were spot on for the subjects that would be in people's minds.

But where does the Bible say that rivers of living water will flow out of people's hearts? (The word used here properly means 'stomachs' or 'bellies', but it's clearly referring to the deepest parts of the personality, and today we normally say 'heart' when we mean that.) The only passage which seems to fit is the long final section of the prophet Ezekiel, and particularly chapter 47.

There, as part of the prophet's great vision of the **Temple** and Jerusalem wonderfully restored after the **exile**, there is a description of how a new river will flow from under the Temple threshold. It will get deeper and deeper, and will make its way down to the Dead Sea – past the spot where I stood that day overlooking the Qumran settlement. When it reaches the Dead Sea, it will make it fresh, so that people will fish in it and wonderful fruit trees will grow all around it. This is the same picture that is used at the end of the Revelation of St John (22.1–2), as part of the description of the New Jerusalem.

The promise of these verses is therefore staying quite close to what we saw in chapter 4. Instead of a new city and Temple, Jesus is suggesting that the promise will be fulfilled in individual human beings. Standing there in the Temple, perhaps at the time when the priests were solemnly pouring water out around the altar in thanksgiving for God's blessing and in hope for the future, Jesus shouts out his invitation to anyone, anyone at all, who wants to have the water of life bubbling up inside them, and flowing out to the world around.

John's comment helps us to hold this promise in the right framework. Jesus was speaking, he says, about the **spirit**; anyone who believes in Jesus is promised that the spirit, God's refreshing personal presence, will come to live within them. But John knew, too, that this was a new experience that would come after Jesus had been 'glorified'.

What does this mean? It seems clearly to refer to Jesus' death; and from now on John will refer to his forthcoming crucifixion more and more in these terms. This fits with what he said before about the crucifixion as a 'lifting up' of Jesus (3.14): he will be physically 'lifted up' on the cross, but this will also be his moment of true glory. Only through the work of the cross, in which God's lamb takes away the sins of the world, can human hearts be made clean and fit, like a renewed and rebuilt Temple, for the spirit to flood them to overflowing in the way God longs to do.

The moment of Jesus' death is coming steadily closer. We can feel, in this passage, the pressure of opposition building up and Jesus being aware of it and responding. He is going away, he says. They misunderstand, as usual – and yet it isn't a complete misunderstanding, because when Jesus is 'glorified' there will indeed be Greeks who come to **faith** in him (see, too, 12.20–23). But just as Jesus has a unique promise for all who are thirsty, so he has a unique vocation through which he will bring it about. He is the one true spirit-giver, because he is the one and only lamb of God who gives himself, in glorious love, for the sins of the world.

JOHN 7.40–52

Where Does the Messiah Come From?

⁴⁰When they heard these words, some people in the crowd said, 'This man really is "the Prophet"!'

⁴¹'He's the Messiah!' said some others.

But some of them replied, 'The Messiah doesn't come from Galilee, does he? ⁴²Doesn't the Bible say that the Messiah is descended from David, and comes from Bethlehem, the city where David was?'

⁴³So there was a division in the crowd because of him. ⁴⁴Some of them wanted to arrest him, but nobody laid hands on him.

⁴⁵So the servants went back to the chief priests and the Pharisees. 'Why didn't you get him?' they asked.

⁴⁶'No man ever spoke like this!' the servants replied.

⁴⁷'You don't mean to say you've been taken in too?' answered the Pharisees. ⁴⁸'None of the rulers or the Pharisees have believed in him, have they? ⁴⁹But this rabble that doesn't know the law – a curse on them!'

⁵⁰Nicodemus, who went to Jesus earlier, and who was one of their own number, spoke up.

⁵¹'Our law doesn't condemn a man, does it, unless first you hear his side of the story and find out what he's doing?'

⁵²'Oh, so you're from Galilee too, are you?' they answered him. 'Check it out and see! No prophet ever rises up from Galilee!'

I watched in admiration as the chess game reached its closing stages. Somehow the television commentator managed to explain what the two master players were doing in such a way that even a complete beginner like myself could understand. The younger man would make a move; the commentator would explain how brilliant it was, how unexpected and yet how devastating and powerful. Then, after a due pause, the older player would respond, and again the commentator would explain how, though you couldn't have predicted it, and certainly his opponent wouldn't have imagined he would do that, this was in fact the perfect, teasing answer. So it went on, with two great minds trying to outthink each other, and us mere watchers being helped to understand the plot and counterplot, the multiple layers of strategy, going on all the time.

We need that kind of help with a passage like this, because in almost every line John is inviting us to watch a sequence of comments that are almost like the moves in a chess game. The point, too, is the same: where is the king, and can we capture him?

The opening moves pick up from the rest of the chapter, and of the book. Is Jesus 'the prophet', the one like Moses, promised in Deuteronomy 18? (See John 1.21 and 6.14.) Is he the **Messiah** himself? But, if he is, there's a problem about his origins. This is the only time in John's **gospel** that either Bethlehem or David is mentioned, though John almost certainly knew the traditions which we find in Matthew and Luke, according to which Jesus was born in Bethlehem, though spending most of his early years in Galilee. It may be that here already John intends that his readers, whom he expects to know those stories or others like them, will have a sense of looking over the shoulders of the chess players and seeing them miss something.

But he doesn't develop the point. He goes back to the servants who had been sent earlier to arrest Jesus (verse 32), and we find that they have come back without him. Their employers, the **priests**, are angry: they were sent to do a job, and they haven't done it. The servants, though, have an answer ready: nobody ever heard anyone speaking like Jesus was speaking. (People still say that today, often enough, when they really settle down to read what he said.) They were stunned by him.

But the **Pharisees** have an answer for that. Anybody with any knowledge of the Jewish **law** should know that this fellow is out of line! (So far the only law Jesus even seems to have broken, as far as John's gospel is concerned, is the **sabbath**; but they clearly regard his action as indicating a casual approach to the whole thing.) They dismiss, with a contemptuous wave of the hand, the 'rabble that doesn't know the law', the mass of ordinary Jews who hadn't studied **Torah** in detail, or who held less stringent views of it than did the Pharisees themselves. As far as they are concerned, such people are effectively under God's curse. If God has revealed his will in the law, and if people don't take the trouble to understand it and follow it, so much the worse for them! No wonder they're taken in by a deceitful would-be prophet with a smooth tongue!

The answer looks devastating. But then the next move in the chess match turns the game the other way again. John introduces us again to

Nicodemus, who had come to Jesus by night (3.1–13), and whom we now discover to be at least sitting on the fence. By 19.39 we discover that he has become a **disciple**; perhaps his disgust at his colleagues in this passage had something to do with pushing him towards full **faith** in Jesus. His response shows that, in fact, if anyone round here doesn't know the law it's the Pharisees themselves! They are condemning Jesus without having heard what he has to say for himself or seen what he is doing. They are behaving in the classic manner of people who are threatened by a new idea: reject it quickly, on whatever pretext comes to hand. People still do this with the gospel, alas, and we still need Nicodemuses to point out the fallacy in what is so often said.

The chess game isn't over, though: they think they have an answer for him. The sarcasm ('You're from Galilee too, are you?', when they know perfectly well he isn't) shows what's really at stake: they are looking down their noses not just at the majority of ordinary Jews in Jerusalem because they don't follow their teaching, but also at the people who come from up north.

And, as John surely intends us to see, their point about prophets not coming from Galilee shows just how wrong they are. Jonah and Hosea, two well-known prophets in the Old Testament, both came from Galilee. And when John has them say that no prophet 'rises up' from Galilee, the word he uses is almost always used elsewhere in the book to refer to the **resurrection**. Jonah was proverbial for coming, so it seemed, back 'from the dead' after three days in the belly of the fish; and Hosea contains the prophecy that God will 'raise us up on the third day' (6.2).

Not only, then, are the Pharisees wrong about prophets coming from Galilee. The very language they use points to the truth, that Jesus not only 'arises' from there as his homeland, but will also 'rise up' in a far deeper sense, proving that he is indeed 'the prophet' and the Messiah. John intends that we, watching this extraordinary verbal chess match, should be able to tell which king is going to win in the end.

JOHN 7.53–8.11

Adultery and Hypocrisy

[53]They all went off home,
[1]and Jesus went to the Mount of Olives. [2]In the morning he went back to the Temple. All the people came to him, and he sat down and taught them.

[3]The scribes and Pharisees brought a woman who had been caught out in adultery. They stood her out in the middle.

[4]'Teacher,' they said to him. 'This woman was caught in the very act of adultery. [5]In the law, Moses commanded us to stone people like this. What do you say?'

⁶They said this to test him, so that they could frame a charge against him.

Jesus squatted down and wrote with his finger on the ground. ⁷When they went on pressing the question, he got up and said to them,

'Whichever of you is without sin should throw the first stone at her.'

⁸And once again he squatted down and wrote on the ground.

⁹When they heard that, they went off one by one, beginning with the oldest. Jesus was left alone, with the woman still standing there.

¹⁰Jesus looked up.

'Where are they, woman?' he asked. 'Hasn't anybody condemned you?'

¹¹'Nobody, sir,' she replied.

'Well, then,' said Jesus, 'I don't condemn you either! Off you go – and from now on don't sin again!'

Two women were brought before the young king. They were prostitutes, and shared a house. Both had given birth, but the son of one of them had died. Now both were claiming the living son as their own. How could anyone tell (in the days before DNA testing!) which one was speaking the truth?

The king gave his judgment. Bring a sword, he said, and cut the boy in two. Each woman can have half of him.

The instant reaction of the two women told him the truth. One of them agreed with the verdict. The other one begged that the boy should live, even if her rival was allowed to keep him. No question which was the true mother.

The king was, of course, Solomon; the story is told in 1 Kings 3.16–28. It was the kind of thing that got him his reputation for remarkable wisdom. And this is the kind of story that people in the first century would think of when they heard this story about Jesus, the woman taken in adultery, and the men taken in . . . hypocrisy.

There is a puzzle about this story. It doesn't really seem to fit here. Chapters 7 and 8 – omitting this passage – seem to flow on reasonably well. And, tellingly, the earliest copies of John's **gospel** do in fact run straight on from 7.52 to 8.12, missing this story out altogether. At the same time, some manuscripts put it in, but in a different place. Some have it as an extra story after the end of the gospel. Some even place it in Luke's gospel (and it has to be said that the way the story is told is, if anything, more like Luke than like John). That's why some translations of the Bible put the story in brackets, or add it to the end as an 'appendix'.

At the same time, there is something to be said for reading it here, where a lot of manuscripts do have it. John 7 has Jesus teaching in the **Temple** during the festival of Tabernacles, and the crowds and authorities getting increasingly interested in asking who he is and what he's about. John 8 has an altogether darker tone, with Jesus accusing the Judaeans of wilfully misunderstanding him, failing to grasp what he's saying, and wanting to kill him, because they are following the dictates of 'their father, the **devil**'. Chapter 8 contains some of the harshest things Jesus is ever recorded as saying. What has happened?

It is as though Jesus has come face to face with the real problem at the heart of the Judaean attitude – to him, to God, to themselves, to their national vocation. We won't understand the chapter if we think of the Judaeans as simply interested bystanders trying to make sense of a curious teacher newly arrived in town. If we read it like that, Jesus appears irrationally angry and dismissive, and indeed that's what they seem to have thought too (see verses 48 and 52). John, writing the chapter, is well aware of the impression Jesus was making.

The chapter fits, in other words, with a change of mood brought on by something which has caught Jesus' attention, and has made him realize just how steeped in their own patterns of thinking his Judaean contemporaries had become – and how devastatingly unlike God's patterns of thinking they were. So, whether or not the story of the woman and her accusers originally belonged here, it certainly helps us to understand the chapter which it now introduces. The chapter as it now stands begins with people wanting to stone a woman to death; it ends with them wanting to stone Jesus. Perhaps that, too, is trying to tell us something.

The story is a classic example of Jesus' own wisdom, the sort of wisdom that kings were expected to display. (Remember that the underlying question of this whole part of John's gospel is whether or not Jesus is the **Messiah**, the true king.) The story turns on the trap that the **scribes** and **Pharisees** had set for Jesus. They suspected that he would want to tell the woman that her sins had been forgiven; but that would mean that he would be teaching people to ignore something in the **law** of Moses.

Already we can sense the temperature of the situation rising, and with it Jesus' anger. They are using the woman, however guilty she might be of serious sin, simply as a tool in their attack on him. And, in so doing, they are enjoying their sense of moral superiority over her, as well as their sense of having put Jesus in a corner he can't easily escape from.

Nobody knows, of course, what Jesus was writing on the ground. (In the ancient world, teachers often used to write or draw in the dust; that's how some of the great geometry teachers would explain things, in the days before chalkboards and overhead projectors.) We can guess if we like; maybe he was writing lists of other sins, including hypocrisy. Maybe he was making a point about sins of the eye and heart, as in

80

Matthew 5.28. Or maybe he was just doodling, treating their question with the contempt it deserved.

But his answer when it came, though apparently risky (supposing one of them had had the arrogance to go ahead?), was devastating. When you point the finger at someone else, there are three fingers pointing back at you. He hasn't said the law of Moses was wrong; only that, if we're going to get serious about it, we should all find ourselves guilty. And one by one they get the point and go away.

The story certainly doesn't mean – as some people have tried to make it mean – that adultery doesn't matter. That's not the point at all. Jesus' last words to the woman are extremely important. If she has been forgiven – if she's been rescued from imminent death – she must live by that forgiveness. *Forgiveness is not the same thing as 'tolerance'.* Being forgiven doesn't mean that sin doesn't matter. On the contrary: 'forgiveness' means that sin *does* matter – but that God is choosing to set it aside.

And the sin that matters even more, as the rest of the chapter makes clear, is the deep-rooted sin which uses the God-given law as a means of making oneself out to be righteous, when in fact it is meant to shine the light of God's judgment into the dark places of the heart. By confronting this sin, Jesus has put himself, literally, in the firing line from which he has just rescued the woman. If you read chapter 8 as it stands from beginning to end you may start to see a pattern which will continue through to Jesus' death. This is part of what it means, John seems to be saying, that Jesus is God's lamb, the one who takes away the sin of the world.

JOHN 8.12–20

The Light of the World

[12]Jesus spoke to them again.

'I am the light of the world,' he said. 'People who follow me won't go around in the dark; they'll have the light of life!'

[13]'You're giving evidence in your own case!' said the Pharisees. 'Your evidence is false!'

[14]'Even if I do give evidence about myself,' replied Jesus to them, 'my evidence is true, because I know where I came from and where I'm going to. But you don't know where I come from or where I'm going to. [15]You are judging in merely human terms; I don't judge anyone. [16]But even if I do judge, my judgment is true, because I'm not a lone voice; I have on my side the father who sent me. [17]It is written in your law that the evidence of two people is true. [18]I'm giving evidence about myself, and the father who sent me is giving evidence about me.'

[19]'Where is your father?' they said to him.

'You don't know me,' replied Jesus, 'and you don't know my father! If you had known me, you would have known my father as well.' [20]He said all this in the treasury, while he was teaching in the Temple. Nobody arrested him, though, because his time hadn't yet come.

As we turned the corner, we saw a large yellow sign beside the road. The two words that jumped out at us were 'ACCIDENT' and 'WITNESS'.

It appeared there had been a road accident at that dangerous corner the previous Friday night. Some people had been badly hurt, and a considerable amount of expensive damage had been done. And the police didn't know who was responsible. They were appealing for more witnesses to come forward. Had anyone seen anything? Did anyone know anything? It was no good asking the people who were hurt. They were bound to say it wasn't their fault. They were bound to blame someone else. If the case was to go ahead – if truth was to come out, and justice was to be done – the police would need more witnesses, and independent ones at that.

That is where we are in this passage. Once again we are back in court. But who is on trial?

It looks, to begin with, as though it's Jesus. The **Pharisees**, having failed in their attempt to bring a charge against him for setting aside the **law** of Moses (8.5), are now examining the claims he appears to be making. And much of the discussion seems to turn on a legal point: is the defendant allowed to give evidence in his own case, or must we assume that to do so is invalid? Jesus, for his part, is insisting on his right to give evidence about himself, but claiming that this evidence is backed up by the father who sent him. As Nicodemus had said earlier on, nobody could do the works that Jesus was doing unless God was with them (3.2). Jesus points out to the Pharisees that the law itself specifies two witnesses: well, he and the father count together as two, don't they?

This isn't the last word on the subject; the question of evidence and conviction continues to haunt the **gospel** right through until the moment when Jesus stands before Pilate in chapter 19. But as we look at the present passage we may start to wonder if we've got the trial the right way round.

The claim which Jesus makes at the start comes as a bolt from the blue. This is so, whether verse 12 is meant to follow on from the story of the hypocrites and the adulteress in 7.53–8.11, or whether it runs straight on from 7.52. John has told us, of course, that '**life** was in him, and this life was the light of the human race' (1.4), and he went on to speak of the light shining in darkness, and the darkness not overcoming it. Later on, we saw that the difference between good and evil could be seen in terms of goodness coming to the light and evil shunning it, in case it should be exposed (3.19–21). And that sets the terms for part at least of the present passage.

The idea of God calling someone to be the means of bringing light to the world is rooted in ancient Judaism. There, in the prophet Isaiah in particular, it is Israel who will be the world's true light. But, ultimately, it is the Lord's servant who is anointed to bring God's truth and justice to the world, and who at the climax of the book dies a cruel death to achieve the goal (Isaiah 42.6; 49.6; 53.1—12; 60.1, 3). The claim to be the world's true light, like so much that Jesus says in this gospel, is not in itself a claim to be divine (though John believes that, and wants us to believe it too); it is a claim to be Israel's **Messiah**. It is, in principle, a claim that we can imagine other would-be Messiahs of the period making. After all, the last great would-be Messiah in this period was Simeon ben-Kosiba, who led a revolution in AD 132–35, and who became known as bar-Kochba, 'son of the star'. He was, so his followers believed, a great light sent from **heaven**.

But the light that God intends to bring illumination to the whole world is the same light that shines relentlessly into the world's dark corners. And when it does so it brings judgment. Throughout the gospel it's clear that Jesus had not basically come to judge the world, or Israel, or individuals; but it's also clear that the fact of his coming to bring rescue, salvation, life and hope would inevitably have the effect of condemning those who didn't want any of those things, those who were so steeped in evil that the coming of light was bad news for them, not good news.

So, gradually, we begin to realize that when the witnesses are brought in this case it is not Jesus who is really on trial. It is those who are opposing him. He and his father are giving evidence that he is the Messiah; but, if this is so, he is bringing the light that they cannot escape. As he has come to realize, at the heart of the Israel of his day there was a single great problem: they had forgotten who their God really was. Their behaviour, their attitudes and their ambitions indicated that they didn't know the one Jesus called 'father'; and that was why they couldn't recognize him as having come from this one true God.

This highlights the problem which runs through the whole chapter. Israel was supposed to be the light of the world; but Israel was providing only darkness. If Jesus was now shining the true light into that darkness, there could only be one result: a head-on clash. That is what we find.

Are you ever tempted to reject the light? As you read John 8, do you ever find yourself siding with the Pharisees? Have we all, perhaps, allowed ourselves to forget just how deep the darkness goes within each of us, not least when we are called to be God's people for the world but decide to turn this calling into a privilege for ourselves?

JOHN 8.21-29 From Below or from Above

JOHN 8.21–29

From Below or from Above

²¹So Jesus spoke to them once more.

'I am going away,' he said. 'You will look for me, and you will die in your sin. You can't come where I'm going.'

²²'Is he going to kill himself?' asked the Judaeans. 'Is that what he means when he says we can't come where he's going?'

²³'You come from below,' Jesus said to them, 'but I come from above. You are from this world, I am not from this world. ²⁴I told you that you would die in your sins; you see, that's what will happen to you if you don't believe that I am the one.'

²⁵'Who are you?' they asked.

'What I've been telling you from the beginning,' replied Jesus. ²⁶'There are plenty of things I could say about you, yes, and against you too! But the one who sent me is true, and I tell the world what I heard from him.'

²⁷They didn't understand that he was talking about the father.

²⁸So Jesus said to them, 'When you've lifted up the son of man, then you will know that I'm the one, and that I never act on my own initiative; I say exactly what the father taught me. ²⁹And the one who sent me is with me. He hasn't left me alone, because I always do what pleases him.'

'The house is on fire! Get up at once!'

She burst into the dormitory where several of the other girls were sleeping. She dashed to the nearest bed and shook the sleeper violently.

'Come on! There's no time! You'll be burnt alive!'

'Go back to sleep!' came the reply. 'It's just one of your stupid nightmares! Stop making a nuisance of yourself!'

'Well, I'm going out right now!' she said. 'And if you don't come with me, you'll all be fried in your beds!'

Would you believe someone shouting at you in the middle of the night? Well, it might depend on whether you trusted them anyway. You might at least think it was worth finding out. But finding out meant getting out of bed on a cold night; and that meant waking up properly, when what you most wanted was to drift straight back off to sleep.

Jesus is offering his contemporaries a last chance to change, to trust him, to act on his warnings, and so to escape the fate that is otherwise going to come on them. When we read a sentence like 'you will die in your sin', most of us naturally imagine that it refers only to an inward, spiritual condition, a spiritual death that takes place inside the heart and soul, and the spiritual death that takes place at, or after, physical death for those who have resolutely turned their back on God.

84

But in the other **gospels** we can see that Jesus' warnings also have a more specific reference, to events that were taking place in his own day, to the great crisis and devastation that was building up in the Middle East. Echoes of this find their way into John as well: in chapter 11, Caiaphas warns his fellow-leaders that if they're not careful the Romans will come and destroy the holy city altogether. That is the threat that's hanging over Jesus' contemporaries; they know it and so does he. So when he warns them that 'they will die in their sins', it is highly likely that he has this danger, not only the danger of personal or spiritual annihilation, in mind.

But he is offering an alternative! If they would only believe that he is the **Messiah**, sent by God to rescue Israel and the world, then they would be able to follow him and not plunge into ruin. But Jesus already knows that they won't. He has seen enough to realize that the Judaeans, by and large, are set against any appeal such as the one he is making.

The result is that Jesus himself won't be with them for long. He will 'go away'. The Judaeans rightly deduce that he means he's going to die, and to die quite soon; but they can't see how it will happen. We know that there have already been threats against Jesus' life, and at the end of this passage (verse 28) Jesus suggests that they themselves will 'lift up' the **son of man** – in other words, that they or their rulers and leaders will bear some responsibility at least for his execution at the hands of the pagan Romans. He will be rejected by his own people, because his **message** is completely unpalatable. He has come to his own, and his own will not receive him.

Imagine someone going into public life today, who dreams of serving his country. He has high ideals, believes in working for justice in society and sees himself persuading people to follow him in a gentle process leading to greater prosperity for all. Then, at the very point where our hero becomes prime minister, the world suddenly erupts into a violent war. Many in the nation want to take one side; some are convinced they should support the others. What is a leader to do in this situation? What happens to all the ideals of steadily building a better society? When there's a crisis, nettles have to be grasped, difficult decisions have to be made, opponents have to be confronted.

We would prefer to think of Jesus teaching, in a friendly fashion, people (like we imagine ourselves to be, perhaps) who simply want to listen and learn, who want truth and wisdom to live by, who are looking for the secret of the gospel of salvation. But this passage indicates that life was seldom if ever like that during Jesus' public career. There was little time, especially in Jerusalem, for leisurely teaching, for pondering deep timeless truths. Things were urgent; the chief **priests** and

Pharisees, and those whom they influenced, were either going to listen to him or they weren't.

And Jesus increasingly realized that they weren't. Despite the fact that they were God's people, they were 'from below'; they simply didn't understand how the God of whom he spoke could be the same as the God they thought they knew. This is the tragedy at the heart of the story of Jesus, in all four gospels. And, like everything else, it reaches its height on the cross. When Jesus is 'lifted up', then and only then everything becomes clear.

Where is your country heading at the moment? Where is your life heading at the moment? What difference should believing that Jesus is God's anointed one make to either of them?

JOHN 8.30–36

The Truth Will Make You Free

[30]As Jesus said all this, several people believed in him.

[31]So Jesus spoke to the Judaeans who had believed in him.

'If you remain in my word,' he said, 'you will truly be my disciples. [32]You will know the truth, and the truth will make you free.'

[33]'We are Abraham's descendants!' they replied. 'We've never been anyone's slaves! How can you say that "You'll become free"?'

[34]'I'm telling you the solemn truth,' Jesus replied. 'Everyone who commits sin is a slave of sin. [35]The slave doesn't live in the house for ever; the son lives there for ever. [36]So, you see, if the son makes you free, you will be truly free.'

The square was crowded. Indeed, it was more than crowded: it was packed to overflowing. People were leaning from windows in the beautifully sculpted office blocks around the square. It was lunchtime, but nobody was thinking of eating. There must have been at least a hundred thousand people in all, and they were all singing.

I remember it vividly. It was the first time I'd ever been in such a crowd. It was in Nathan Phillips Square in the heart of Toronto, and it was 5 April 1968 – the day after Martin Luther King Jr. had been assassinated. As far as I remember, the demonstration wasn't organized; it just happened. And everyone was singing 'We Shall Overcome'.

We sang it a lot in those days. It became a sort of anthem of the black liberation movement, but it went a lot wider too. It was part of the whole 1960s sea change that came over Western society, as those of us who had grown up in the years after the Second World War began to look around us and ask why so many things in society were still so wrong. But it also had – as Martin Luther King himself would have wanted to give it – a specifically biblical and Christian message. Freedom was part of what the **gospel** had promised. It wasn't just a promise for freedom from this world, for a new **life** after death. It was a promise about freedom in the here and now.

One of the verses we regularly sang was taken from this passage in St John: 'the truth will set you free'. Verse 32 rings like a great bell through so much Christian language: free from sin, free from slavery, free from the **law**, free from death, free from injustice, free from debt, free from tyranny. It's needed today as much as ever, in all of these senses and more. The way to freedom is through the truth, and what matters therefore is to know the truth. Tyranny and slavery of every sort thrive on lies, half-truths, evasions and cover-ups. Freedom and truth go hand in hand.

So Jesus is offering – we might have thought – what everybody in Israel was longing for! Freedom at last! And at an even deeper level than they had imagined. Surely this will catch people's attention, especially with those who, as John says, have now come to believe that he really is the **Messiah** (verse 30)?

Surprisingly, no. They hear straight away that he is offering a freedom which goes far beyond the national hope of freedom from Rome, and they react against the idea. 'How can you say such a thing? We are Abraham's children, and we've always been free!'

Jesus doesn't point out, as he might have done, that the foundation of their national life and **faith** was not just Abraham, but the **Exodus** which had taken place after their slavery in Egypt. He goes straight to the heart of what he means. There is a worse slavery than that which they had suffered in Egypt, or the semi-slavery they were suffering under the rule of Rome. It is the slavery that grips not only individuals but also groups, nations and families of nations. It is the slavery we know as 'sin'.

The trouble with saying that out loud is that many people in the Western world are bored of hearing about sin. They think it just means offences against someone else's old-fashioned morality, often in matters to do with sex. But that's far too small-minded a view. Sexual sins matter, of course; they matter very much. They can destroy a person, a marriage, a family, a community. But there is more to sin than sex, and sin as a whole is far greater than the sum of its parts. When people rebel against God in whatever way, new fields of force are called into being, a cumulative effect builds up, and individuals and societies alike become enslaved just as surely as if every single one of them wore chains and was hounded to work every day by a strong man with a whip.

So what is the truth, and how can it set people free, then and now?

Throughout John's gospel, with 1.14, 18 and 14.6 as particular high points, the answer is clear: Jesus himself is the truth. But we mustn't forget that the Jesus who is described as the truth is the Jesus of the whole story John is telling, and above all the Jesus who dies on the cross as the supreme act of love, the act in which the father's glory is finally revealed.

Jesus doesn't here explain how it is that his death – the truth within the truth, if you like – brings about freedom from sin. To understand this promise you have to read the whole gospel. But he does point out, in verses 35–36, the contrast between the slave and the son – and between the slave and the ex-slave, the one whom the son sets free. It forms a solemn warning. Slaves have no assurance for the future; only true members of the family have that. Jesus, as the father's only, special son (1.18), is in a position not only to set people free but to share with them his status as children of the father (see 20.17).

The charge Jesus is putting to his contemporaries, then, is that they are confusing two sorts of family membership: being children of Abraham and being children of God. They have been assuming that being children of Abraham means automatically being children of God, but **John the Baptist**, Jesus and the early Christians, especially writers like John and Paul, insisted that this wasn't so. In fact, they insisted that the children of Abraham had been deeply and seriously infected by the disease of sin, the disease of which the rest of the human race was already suffering. The people called to bring God's light to the world were instead sharing in the darkness. But there was still a chance. If only they would hear and receive Jesus' words, they could themselves be set free from the slavery they didn't even know they were in.

The same is true today, not least when people assume that nominal membership of a Christian church means they are automatically in God's favour. What if the people called to carry Jesus' light into the world are themselves infected with darkness?

JOHN 8.37–47

Children of Abraham – or of the Devil

[37]'I know you're Abraham's descendants,' Jesus went on. 'But you're trying to kill me, because my word doesn't find a place among you. [38]I am speaking of what I have seen with the father; and you, too, are doing what you heard from your father.'

[39]'Abraham is our father!' they replied.

'If you really were Abraham's children,' replied Jesus, 'you would do what Abraham did! [40]But now you're trying to kill me – me, a man

88

who has told you the truth which I heard from God! That's not what Abraham did. [41]'You're doing the works of *your* father.'

'There wasn't anything immoral about the way *we* were born!' they replied. 'We've got one father, and that's God!'

[42]'If God really was your father,' replied Jesus, 'you would love me, because I came from God, and here I am. I didn't come on my own initiative, you see, but he sent me. [43]Why don't you understand what I'm saying? It can only be because you can't hear my word. [44]You are from your father – the devil! And you're eager to get on with what he wants. He was a murderer from the beginning, and he's never remained in the truth, because there is no truth in him. When he tells lies, he speaks what comes naturally to him, because he is a liar – in fact, he's the father of lies! [45]But because I speak the truth, you don't believe me. [46]Which of you can bring a charge of sin against me? If I speak the truth, why don't you believe me? [47]The one who is from God speaks God's words. That's why you don't listen, because you're not from God.'

The famous psychologist Carl Jung published, among his many works, a picture-book illustrating the main points of his thought about the strange ways in which the human mind works. One of the most striking pages is a picture of Adolf Hitler. Underneath is a caption which reads something like this: 'This man is going to set all Europe ablaze with his incendiary dreams of world domination!'

The reader glances at this, and thinks: Well, yes, of course. That is what happened. Hitler's much-publicized ambition of founding a German empire that would last for a thousand years did indeed lead directly both to the Second World War and to the slaughter of millions of Jews (as well as gypsies and others he considered 'undesirable'). But then Jung points out that the caption was in fact what Adolf Hitler said about Winston Churchill. Jung gives it as an example of 'projection', when you accuse somebody else of the thing you are guilty of yourself.

That is just one example of the way in which powerful lies can be invented and can spread in people's minds. In his remarkable novel *The Portage to San Cristabel of A. H.*, the Jewish writer George Steiner takes the same theme further, imagining a small group of Jewish Nazi-hunters discovering the aged Hitler in the far recesses of the South American swamps, and bringing him out to face whatever justice there could be. The climax of the book is Hitler's astonishing speech in his own defence, in which he not only claims that other regimes made his genocide look tame by comparison, but also accuses the Jewish people themselves of having invented the idea of world domination and of killing other nations to make it possible. Perhaps only a Jewish writer, and a deeply sensitive one at that, would have dared not only to write such a thing, but also to bring the novel to a close without any attempt to refute the charge, leaving it to the reader to think through how and why Hitler's brilliant oratory was in fact a tissue of lies, half-truths and gross misrepresentations from start to finish.

It is the memory of Hitler's unspeakable atrocities, based on the ultimate lie that Jews were an inferior species and that it was a moral duty to obliterate them, that has given readers of this passage so much trouble. It looks as though the Jesus of John chapter 8 is accusing 'the Jews' in general of being the children of the **devil**, of being inveterate liars and murderers. We instinctively recoil, and wonder if this can be the Jesus we know and love from the rest of the New Testament.

This is understandable, but it is an overreaction. We prefer – at least, the liberal-minded Western world prefers – to think of Jesus and his teaching in terms of sweet gentleness and reasonableness, helping people to understand the love of God by homely illustrations and **parables** drawn from everyday life. This sharp exchange is an embarrassment at the level of culture, almost of good manners.

But we need to think again. The chapter is about a man facing a mob. Some of their leaders and opinion-formers have already decided that he is leading Israel astray and ought to be killed. Several of them are ready to get on with the job immediately. A party had already been sent to arrest him, but had failed to do so (7.30–32, 44–46). The crowd in front of him now were ready to stone him (verse 59). This is no gentle, devotional discussion of deep personal religious truth, set within a framework of civility and mutual respect: this is a man facing a crowd set upon lynching him, and bravely speaking up against their hypocrisy. It should hardly need saying that the 'Judaeans' here are not intended to represent 'Jews' in general, then or now. Jesus and his followers were after all Jewish as well, and so were people like Nicodemus who had already begun to follow him (7.50). The 'Judaeans' are the first-century Jerusalemites, to whom Jesus came as 'his own', and who did not receive him (1.11).

Jesus' basic charge against them is that they are trying to kill him; that this shows that they do not know the God whom he knows as his father; and that this in turn shows that their boast to be children of Abraham is spurious. When someone is bent upon murder, they are thereby disclaiming descent from the true God, and are silently claiming instead that they belong to the forces of darkness. However we imagine the devil, it is clear that there is a force which opposes God and his good creation, which drives people to commit acts of destruction and murder, and which regularly invents lies – the 'religious' ones are often the most effective – to excuse such action, and even to make it appear noble and right. There are plenty of these in today's world, including (alas) several that call themselves Christian. If we want to see where this passage applies most obviously to today's world this is where we should start.

The response of the Judaeans in verse 41 suggests that people already knew, during Jesus' lifetime, the fact that there was something strange about the circumstances of his conception and birth. Though John doesn't tell us the story of Jesus' birth in the way that Matthew and Luke do, when we take this passage with the hint some have seen in 1.13, it may appear that he, too, knew of it – and that some of Jesus' opponents were already using it as a sneer against him.

JOHN 8.48-59

Before Abraham, 'I Am'

⁴⁸This was the Judaeans' response to Jesus.

'Haven't we been right all along,' they said, 'in saying you're a Samaritan, and that you've got a demon inside you?'

⁴⁹'I haven't got a demon!' replied Jesus. 'I am honouring my father, and you are dishonouring me. ⁵⁰I'm not looking for my own glory; there is one who is looking after that, and he will be the judge. ⁵¹I'm telling you the solemn truth: anyone who keeps my word will never, ever see death.'

⁵²'Now we know that you really *have* got a demon!' replied the Judaeans. 'Look here: Abraham died! So did the prophets! And here are you, saying, "Anyone who keeps my word will never, ever taste death." ⁵³You're not suggesting, are you, that you're greater than our father Abraham? He died, and so did the prophets! Who are you making yourself out to be?'

⁵⁴'If I do give myself glory,' replied Jesus, 'my glory is nothing. My father is the one who brings me glory – the one you say is "our God"; ⁵⁵and you don't know him! I know him, though. If I were to say I didn't know him, I would be a liar like you. But I do know him, and I keep his word. ⁵⁶Your father Abraham celebrated the fact that he would see my day. He saw it and was delighted.'

⁵⁷'You're not yet fifty years old!' responded the Judaeans. 'Have you seen Abraham?'

⁵⁸'I'm telling you the solemn truth,' replied Jesus. 'Before Abraham existed, I Am.'

⁵⁹So they picked up stones to throw at him. But Jesus hid, and left the Temple.

Abraham lived roughly as long before Jesus as Jesus did before us. Speaking of them as in any sense contemporaries conjures up images of time travel, such as has been made famous in the world of science fiction since at least H. G. Wells and Jules Verne, and more recently through movies like the *Back to the Future* series. We have become used at least to holding in our heads the idea that a person from one period in history could somehow be contemporary with a person from a completely different period.

That is the kind of picture we are tempted to think of when we read a passage like this; but it would point us in quite the wrong direction. Jesus isn't saying that Abraham somehow travelled forwards in time to be present when he, Jesus, was alive; nor is he saying that he himself has travelled backwards in time in order to be present with Abraham, two thousand years earlier. He is saying something of a different quality, a different order, altogether.

The Judaeans, who have been getting crosser and more agitated throughout the scene, are clearly ready to take whatever Jesus says and use it in evidence against him. They seem to think that his words do indeed imply that he has been travelling in time, and they mock him for it. He's not yet fifty years old (verse 57), far less five hundred, far less two thousand.

But Jesus is talking at another level altogether. The point he has been making throughout the chapter – the point which is his defence against the capital charge that some are seeking to mount against him for his breaking of the **sabbath** – is that 'the father', Israel's God, the one whom the Judaeans claim to worship, to know and to serve, is operating in and through him in a decisive and unique way, to summon Israel back to a genuine knowledge and allegiance to himself. 'The father' is the one who alone gives **life**; he has given his words to Jesus; so if someone keeps Jesus' words, death will go by them without making any difference (verse 51).

In making claims like this Jesus is not so much talking about himself, but is talking about 'the father who sent me'. This, however, is so striking that his hearers convince themselves that it constitutes evidence of **demon**-possession. (The extra charge that Jesus is a 'Samaritan' is a way of saying 'You're obviously from the wrong tribe altogether – you're bound to be talking nonsense.') All four **gospels** tell us that Jesus' hearers accused him of being either possessed by, or in league with, the **devil** (see Matthew 12.24; Mark 3.22; Luke 11.15). Clearly, this isn't something the early church would have made up; equally clearly, then, Jesus must have been saying and doing things that were remarkable enough, and disturbing enough, to make people throw such an accusation at him. What precisely was he saying here, and why, in the end, did they try to stone him to death?

Jesus could have answered the question of verse 53 by simply saying that God gives life to the faithful departed – a life with him in the present, and a newly embodied life in the **resurrection** to come (see 5.25–29). But he doesn't. He goes further, claiming in verses 54–56 that the one true God is at work in and through him, and that Abraham himself, in trusting this one God and his promises for the future, had celebrated the fact that he would see the day of Jesus. This seems to mean that Abraham, in trusting God's promises that through his family all the peoples of the earth would be blessed, was actually looking ahead to the day when Jesus would bring that promise into reality. He is claiming, in other words, that he, Jesus, is at last embodying what the one living God, Abraham's God, had envisaged and promised all those years ago.

What then does he mean in the crucial verse 58? He is identifying himself so closely with the one true and living God that he can speak of himself as being there 'before Abraham existed'. This is as close as we come on the lips of Jesus to a direct statement of what John says in his Prologue (1.1–2).

Again, we would be wrong to see this passage as part of a gentle, abstract theological discussion. It takes place at the leading edge between ecstasy and fury, with the crowd accusing Jesus of being demon-possessed and Jesus exploring more and more what it means that he is speaking and acting as the very mouthpiece of the father and that they can't and won't understand and believe him. In this setting, what verse 58 seems to mean is this. Jesus is so conscious of the father with him, working in him, speaking through him, that he can speak, in a kind of ecstasy of union, in the name of the father. 'I Am': one of the central meanings of YHWH, the secret and holy name of God. Jesus has seen himself so identified with the father that he can use the Name as a way of referring to himself and his mission. 'Before Abraham existed, I Am'.

The crowd react as predictably as many readers and thinkers have reacted since. In Jesus' own day they accused him of blasphemy, and threatened him with stoning. In our day they accuse him of nonsense ('How can a person be both divine and human?'), and accuse John of making out that Jesus said things which he couldn't have done. John's only answer is to invite us to read on.

JOHN 9.1–12

The Man Born Blind

¹As Jesus was going along, he saw a man who had been blind from birth.

²'Teacher,' his disciples asked him, 'whose sin was it that caused this man to be born blind? Did he sin, or did his parents?'

³'He didn't sin,' replied Jesus, 'nor did his parents. It happened so that God's works could be seen in him. ⁴We must work the works of the one who sent me as long as it's still daytime. The night is coming,

and nobody can work then! [5]As long as I'm in the world, I'm the light of the world.'

[6]With these words, he spat on the ground, and made some mud out of his spittle. He spread the mud on the man's eyes.

[7]'Off you go', he said to him, 'and wash in the pool of Siloam' (which means 'sent'). So he went off and washed. When he came back, he could see.

[8]His neighbours, and the people who used to see him begging, remarked on this.

'Isn't this the man', they said, 'who used to sit here and beg?'
[9]'Yes, it's him!' said some of them.
'No, it isn't!' said some others. 'It's somebody like him.'
But the man himself spoke.
'Yes, it's me,' he said.
[10]'Well, then,' they said to him, 'how did your eyes get opened?'
[11]'It was the man called Jesus!' he replied. 'He made some mud, then he spread it on my eyes, and told me to go to Siloam and wash. So I went, and washed, and I could see!'
[12]'Where is he?' they asked.
'I don't know,' he replied.

I was just waking up, listening to the radio, when a news item caught my attention. Someone had been dismissed from their job for holding heretical views about the afterlife. I listened more intently. Who was it? What job had they been doing? Was it, perhaps, a leading theologian, a bishop even, denying the **resurrection**?

No. It was a football coach. The man then in charge of the England national football squad had said, on the record, that people who suffered from birth defects and disabilities were being punished for sins they had committed in a former life. This is a belief held by some within the broad Hindu tradition (though many Hindus might reject the idea). If you believe in karma, the unstoppable chain of cause and effect running from the present life into a future one, and on to another and another, it is quite conceivable that what someone does in one life will be rewarded, or (as it may be) punished, in another one.

But there was a public outcry. Groups that support the rights of the disabled were, understandably, furious. They raised a storm in the media. And before too long the English football authorities asked the coach to step down from his job. Some people wondered if that was a case of religious discrimination. There was so much confusion among the British media that a few journalists, unable to tell one religion from another, and assuming that any belief in the afterlife was just like any other, described the coach as a 'born-again Christian', by which they seemed to mean 'someone who takes religion seriously'.

In all this confusion, few commentators noticed that there is a passage of the New Testament, namely the present one in John 9, which addresses this very issue. Jesus' **disciples** are Jews. Yet they, and the **Pharisees** in verse 34, assume that there is indeed a connection between present disability and previous sin. The only question then is, whose sin was it? So, faced with a man blind from birth, they deduce that someone must have done something wrong for which this is a punishment.

Thinking like this is a way of trying to hold on to a belief in God's justice. If something in the world seems 'unfair', but if you believe in a God who is both all-powerful, all-loving and all-fair, one way of getting round the problem is to say that it only *seems* 'unfair', but actually isn't. There was after all some secret sin being punished. This is a comfortable sort of thing to believe if you happen to be well-off, well fed and healthy in body and mind. (In other words, if nobody can accuse *you* of some secret previous sin.)

Jesus firmly resists any such analysis of how the world is ordered. The world is stranger than that, and darker than that, and the light of God's powerful, loving justice shines more brightly than that. But to understand it all, we have to be prepared to dismantle some of our cherished assumptions and to let God remake them in a different way.

We have to stop thinking of the world as a kind of moral slot machine, where people put in a coin (a good act, say, or an evil one) and get out a particular result (a reward or a punishment). Of course, actions always have consequences. Good things often happen as a result of good actions (kindness produces gratitude), and bad things often happen through bad actions (drunkenness causes car accidents). But this isn't inevitable. Kindness is sometimes scorned. Some drunkards always get away with it.

In particular, you can't stretch the point back to a previous 'life', or to someone else's sins. Being born blind doesn't mean you must have sinned, says Jesus. Nor does it mean that your parents must have sinned. No: something much stranger, at once more mysterious and more hopeful, is going on. The chaos and misery of this present world is, it seems, the raw material out of which the loving, wise and just God is making his new creation.

When Jesus heals the man, John clearly intends us to see the action as one of the moments in the **gospel** when God's truth and the world's life (theology and history, if you like) come rushing together into one. 'I am the light of the world', says Jesus in verse 5, sending our minds back yet once more to the Prologue: '**life** was in him, and this life was the light of the human race' (1.4). As the passage goes on, we see part of what it means that 'the light shines in the darkness, and the darkness didn't overcome it'. John's gospel is pushing us forward in heart and mind towards God's new creation, the time when God will make all things new.

At the start of the book of Genesis, God was faced with chaos. He didn't waste time describing the chaos, analysing it or discussing whose fault it was. Instead, he created light; and, following the light, a whole new world. So here, John wants us to understand, Jesus is doing 'the works of the one who sent him'. A new chaos is on the way – the 'night', the darkness, when Jesus will be killed and the world will seem to plunge back into primal confusion. But at the moment he is establishing the new world of light and healing. After the chaos of Good Friday and Holy Saturday, he will bring the new creation itself into being with the light of the first Easter Day (John 20.1).

New creation always seems puzzling. Nobody in the story could quite figure out whether the man was the same or not. Sometimes when people receive the **good news** of Jesus it so transforms their lives that people ask the same question: is this really the same person? Can someone who used to lie and steal, to cheat and swear, have become a truthful, wholesome, wise human being? The answer is yes, this can and does happen. In the same way, after Jesus' resurrection, the disciples are faced with the astonishing question: is this really Jesus (20.19–29; 21.4–12)? Again the answer is yes. New creation does happen. Healing does happen. Lives can be transformed. And the question then is the one they asked the man: how did it happen? How *does* it happen?

The answer given throughout the gospel is, of course, 'through Jesus'. And the further question is the one they asked him next: where can we find him?

The man didn't know the answer. But John's whole gospel is written so that we will.

JOHN 9.13–23

The Blind Man's Parents

¹³They took the man who had been blind and brought him to the Pharisees. (¹⁴The day Jesus had made the mud, and opened his eyes, was a sabbath.) ¹⁵So the Pharisees began to ask him again how he had come to see.

'He put some mud on my eyes,' he said, 'and I washed, and now I can see!'

¹⁶'The man can't be from God,' some of the Pharisees began to say. 'He doesn't keep the sabbath!'

'Well, but', replied some of the others, 'how can a man who is a sinner do signs like these?'

And they were divided.

[17]So they spoke to the blind man again.

'What have you got to say about him?' they asked. 'He opened your eyes, after all.'

'He's a prophet', he replied.

[18]The Judaeans didn't believe that he really had been blind and now could see. So they called the parents of the newly sighted man, [19]and put the question to them.

'Is this man really your son,' they asked, 'the one you say was born blind? How is it that he can now see?'

[20]'Well,' replied his parents, 'we know that he is indeed our son, and that he was born blind. [21]But we don't know how it is that he can now see, and we don't know who it was that opened his eyes. Ask him! He's grown up. He can speak for himself.'

[22]His parents said this because they were afraid of the Judaeans. The Judaeans, you see, had already decided that if anyone declared that Jesus was the Messiah, they should be put out of the synagogue. [23]That's why his parents said, 'He's grown up, so you should ask him.'

The street lights weren't working properly that night as my friend walked home late from work. As he took the short cut through the alleyway towards his own street, it was almost pitch dark. He knew the path well enough and wasn't worried about it.

But a moment later he paused. He'd heard a small noise in the darkness just ahead of him. He waited and listened; but, hearing nothing more, he guessed he'd been mistaken and started to walk on. At once he heard the noise again. Again he stopped, and felt a small shiver of fear. What was it? Who was it?

He decided to put on a brave face. 'Who's that?' he asked, hoping his voice didn't sound either too fearful or too threatening.

'Is that you, Peter?' asked the voice of a neighbour. 'Thank goodness! I couldn't see who it was and I was scared stiff!'

Their eyes grew used to the dark and they laughed together. They had both been afraid of each other, quite needlessly.

Many of the world's great problems are like that: two groups in the dark, each afraid of the other. The 'Cold War' between East and West – particularly the Soviet Union and America – in the period from 1945 to 1989 was quite like that. The relationship between Western capitalism and militant Islam is quite like that. Many smaller struggles between religious, cultural and racial groups are like that. The same thing can happen even within the workplace or the home.

Of course, in many cases there are real dangers and threats. Even when the leaders look each other in the eye there may be irreconcilable differences. Sometimes one side really does intend threats against the other. But in many cases fear on one side breeds fear on the other. Fear can breed threats, and sometimes actual violence.

What we have in this passage is the two-way power of fear, acted out as the **Pharisees**, and the parents of the man born blind, try to come to terms with what's just happened.

The Pharisees, it appears, are afraid of something new bursting out within Judaism. They are not afraid in the same way of attack from outside. They are used to that: paganism, the world of non-Jewish religion, money and power, is their ever-present enemy, and they hope that one day God will defeat it. But when people arise from within their Jewish world, claiming to act in the name of the one true God, and start doing things that crack their system from top to bottom, they can't take it.

John, in his **gospel**, has made it easier for us to understand their feelings by his placing of the story of Jesus in the **Temple** early in the gospel, in chapter 2. The leaders in Jerusalem had realized from then on that Jesus was a threat. Once he had healed the cripple on the **sabbath** (chapter 5) they knew more exactly what kind of a threat he was. The disputes that followed in chapters 6, 7 and 8 made this even clearer. Now, we discover, they had settled it that if anyone declared Jesus to be the **Messiah**, they would be put out of the synagogue. (This didn't just mean that they wouldn't be able to join their fellow Judaeans in worship. The synagogue was the focus of the whole community. If you were put out of the synagogue, you'd probably be better off leaving the area altogether.)

This kind of reaction is born of a classic type of fear: fear of the unknown, of something outside the system. The man's parents are also afraid, because they know the threat against anyone saying Jesus is the Messiah. They are anxious for their social standing, their livelihood, perhaps their lives. So anxious, in fact, that they are prepared to let their son face the full brunt of the questioning. 'He's grown up; he can speak for himself.' True, maybe, but hardly the statement of a loving parent.

'Perfect love', says John in one of his letters, 'casts out fear' (1 John 4.18). The gospel story is all about the different ways in which this happens – and the ways in which it doesn't happen when people resist the perfect love which is coming to them in Jesus, coming with God's healing and light. In fact, for John, love and healing are all part of the new creation which is happening in and through Jesus.

New creation speaks of the new 'week'. As we shall see in chapter 20, the **resurrection** is the start of a new week, a new day, the new moment for which the whole world had been longing. The sabbath commanded by Moses speaks of the time of rest at the end of the old creation, the old week. There wasn't anything wrong with the old creation in itself. God saw it and declared it 'very good' (Genesis 1.31). There wasn't anything wrong with the sabbath command in itself (though it's interesting that throughout the New Testament neither Jesus, Paul nor the rest of the early church say anything about Christians being required to keep it). But, as it stood, the sabbath spoke of the old way, in which Israel and the world were still waiting for the new thing God intended to do. The old creation was good, but incomplete. Jesus had come to complete it by making all things new.

The angry, fearful reaction of the Pharisees, and the anxiety of the parents, come together in this sorry tale. Where we would like to see **faith**, acceptance and hope, we see just the opposite. This story speaks to the many dark places in our world today, and no doubt many dark places within our individual lives, where fear, resentment, shock and anxiety cripple our understanding, restrict our faith and stifle our love. The only way through is to follow the small signpost we find in the middle of the passage. The man who had been blind was at least prepared to say that Jesus was a prophet (verse 17). By the end of the story he's moved on to a fuller confession of Jesus as Messiah; but this is a start. When surrounded by fear and anger, the only way through is to glimpse whatever we can see of Jesus, and to follow him out of the dark and into the light.

JOHN 9.24–34

Is Jesus from God?

²⁴So for the second time they called the man who had been blind.

'Give God the glory!' they said. 'We know that this man is a sinner.'

²⁵'I don't know whether he's a sinner or not,' replied the man. 'All I know is this: I used to be blind, and now I can see.'

²⁶'What did he do to you?' they asked. 'How did he open your eyes?'

²⁷'I told you already,' replied the man, 'and you didn't listen. Why d'you want to hear it again? You don't want to become his disciples too, do you?'

²⁸'You're his disciple,' they scoffed, 'but we are Moses's disciples. ²⁹We know that God spoke to Moses, but we don't know where this man comes from.'

³⁰'Well, here's a fine thing!' replied the man. 'You don't know where he's from, and he opened my eyes! ³¹We know that God doesn't listen to sinners; but if anyone is devout, and does his will, he listens to them. ³²It's never, ever been heard of before that someone should open the eyes of a person born blind. ³³If this man wasn't from God, he couldn't do anything.'

| ³⁴'You were born in sin from top to toe,' they replied, 'and are *you* going to start teaching *us*?' And they threw him out.

One of the most depressing things about war is the way in which both sides routinely invoke God on their side. People now joke about the First World War, in which British army chaplains were praying to God for victory while a few hundred yards away the German army chaplains were doing the very same thing. Some have suggested that God must have been very puzzled; others, that God must have a sense of humour, or at least irony, to cope with it. And of course the First World War wasn't the last time the same irony has been seen.

But might there be any way of finding out where God was in such a conflict? Some would say he was absent, forcibly banished by the warmongering forces on either side, greedy for conquest, eager for battle-glory, careless of human life and dignity. Some would say he was present in the hearts and minds of many on both sides who didn't make any great claims about the rightness of their own side's cause, but, finding themselves caught up in events not of their own making, said their prayers and did their duty as they saw it. Some would say he was in the trenches with the wounded and dying, surrounded by mud and blood and stench and death.

As the war of words between Jesus and the Jerusalem hardliners heats up, the question at issue becomes clear: where is God in all of this? The present passage is about healing, about blindness, about Moses and about Jesus; but most of all it's about God.

The **Pharisees** want to drive a solid wedge between Jesus and God. If anything good has happened, they say, it's God's work alone, and Jesus can have had nothing to do with it. The man born blind, no doubt puzzled and afraid (his own parents had retreated from the discussion, leaving him isolated), insists on the reality of his healing, and on Jesus as the cause of it – and hence on the fact that God is indeed at work in and through Jesus. It's a classic case of the difficulty of discovering where God is at work within a controversial event.

The story crackles with irony, as the Pharisees unwittingly say all sorts of things which, from John's point of view, tell against them. 'Give God the glory!' they say to the man born blind – meaning, it seems, 'if you have indeed been healed, it must have been God's doing alone, and nothing to do with Jesus'. But John wants us to see that the man *is* giving God the glory, precisely by sticking to his story and insisting that Jesus had healed him. God must have been working through Jesus, he insists. No other explanation seems possible.

'We know he's a sinner,' they say. They mean, of course, that Jesus appears to have broken the **sabbath** (though whether healing someone, or making clay out of mud and spittle to do so, constituted sabbath-breaking remains dubious). What they mean is this. If Jesus is a sabbath-breaker, and hence a sinner, he can have nothing to do with God. But John wants us to see that Jesus' action in healing the man is the clearest indication that this view of the sabbath is itself wrong. God is doing a new thing, opening up his new world of healing and hope. The Phari-sees' insistence on staying within their own self-imposed interpretation of the **law** only shows how drastically they are themselves out of tune with God's plan.

'We follow Moses,' they say. Yet John wants us to see that Moses spoke of Jesus himself (5.45–47). God did indeed speak through Moses. John wouldn't have denied that for a moment. But when you understand Moses aright, you will see that his law points forward to the 'grace and truth' which comes through Jesus the **Messiah** (1.17). Moses, after all, did far more than merely issue a code of law. He told the *story* of God and Israel, a story with a beginning and a continuation but, as yet, no climac-tic end. John wants us to see that Jesus is himself the climax, the true end of the story – and indeed the beginning of the new story which grows out of the old, and which in turn is now spreading throughout the world.

'You were born in sin from top to toe,' scoff the Pharisees at the man born blind. They have already made their mind up on the question that opened the chapter (9.2–3), the question whether the man's blindness was caused by his own sin or that of his parents. Verse 34 can't mean simply that all human beings are 'born in sin', since that would have meant that the Pharisees were as well. The point they are making is that the man's original physical state was a clear indication of his spiritual state. But John wants us to see not only that his original blindness had nothing to do with his own or his parents' sin, but that Jesus' presence and healing delivers people from everything that's wrong with them, physically, mentally and spiritually.

John wants us to see. Four times we have used that phrase; and that is of course what the passage is all about. It isn't just the man born blind who can now see; it is John's readers, who are being led towards the light which is Jesus himself (9.5; 1.4–5). As throughout the **gospel**, we are meant to look at what Jesus is doing and draw the correct conclusion about the presence of God with and in him. It may be surprising; it may upset some cherished assumptions; it may even be shocking. But when blind eyes are being opened there is only one conclusion to be drawn. Just as Moses shocked the magicians of Egypt by doing things they couldn't copy (Exodus 8.18–19), Jesus is now shocking the world of his

day by doing things for which the only explanation is that God is power-
fully at work. This prepares the way, as did Moses, for the great new **Exodus**, and indeed the great new Genesis, the new creation in which God's
people will be set free not only from blindness but from evil and death.

Being a Christian is often confusing. People try to interpret your
experience for you, to put you in this or that category, to label you.
Often this is so that they needn't take you quite seriously. What you
must do is to stick to what you know. 'I used to be blind; now I can see.'
It may be costly, but paying that cost is better than the still more costly
route of denying what, in Jesus, God has truly done for you.

JOHN 9.35–41

Seeing and Not Seeing

[35]Jesus heard that they had thrown the man out. He found him and
spoke to him.

'Do you believe in the son of man?' he asked.

[36]'Who is he, sir,' asked the man, 'so that I can believe in him?'

[37]'You have seen him,' replied Jesus. 'In fact, it's the person who's
talking to you.'

[38]'Yes, sir,' said the man; 'I do believe.' And he worshipped him.

[39]'I came into the world for judgment,' said Jesus, 'so that those who
can't see would see, and so that those who can see would become
blind.'

[40]Some of the Pharisees were nearby, and they heard this.

'So!' they said. 'We're blind too, are we?'

[41]'If you were blind,' replied Jesus, 'you wouldn't be guilty of sin. But
now, because you say, "We can see", your sin remains.'

Who decides when the picture is in focus?

I attended a lecture the other night in which the speaker showed us
some wonderful colour slides of medieval paintings of Jesus' crucifixion and **resurrection**. The colour was magnificent; the interpretation
was fascinating. But at every point it was up to the lecturer to make
sure that the pictures were in focus so that we could all see everything
clearly. He stood poised and ready with each picture to make the tiny
adjustments that were needed.

This wasn't too difficult. Medieval paintings, full of detail, were
meant to be sharp and visible. But with many modern paintings it
would be different. Sometimes the artist intends things to be fuzzy.
Then it would take someone who understood what the artist was doing
to decide whether things were in focus or not. And if someone said,
'Oh, yes, that's in focus', when it wasn't, everyone would be deceived.

They might think, ever afterwards, that they had understood the painting when they hadn't even seen it properly.

The chapter about the man born blind comes to its conclusion with the complete reversal of where it had started. The chapter began with the **disciples** assuming that because someone was born blind either he or his parents must have been guilty of sin. Jesus opposed that view, healed the man and then warded off the challenge from those who objected to him doing it on the **sabbath**. Now the chapter ends with his accusers claiming to see everything clearly when in fact they can't. And Jesus' comment on their condition is that, though blindness itself isn't an indication of sin, claiming to be able to see when you can't certainly is. 'Because you say, "We can see," your guilt remains' (verse 41).

So the question is: who decides? Who gets to say that the picture is in focus, and what it means? This is, ultimately, a question of authority, a question of judgment. Who has the right to divide the world into those who are seeing clearly and those who are seeing a fuzzy, out-of-focus image of reality which they are mistaking for the real thing?

Here, as always in John, it is Jesus himself who has this right. After he has gone, the same work will be carried on by the **holy spirit**, making Jesus continually present, and bringing his clear judgment to bear on the world (16.8–11). But, during Jesus' ministry it is his own presence, coming as light into the world (9.5, with 3.9–21 and 8.12 in the background), that causes the world to be divided into two. Jesus' presence divides the world into those who come to the light and allow it to change, heal and direct their lives, and those who resist the light and choose to remain in darkness – even while, in some cases, declaring boldly that they see everything clearly.

This work of bringing God's judgment to bear on the world, of setting things to rights and bringing the picture into focus, was often regarded by Jewish thinkers as the proper work of the **Messiah**, the one who would come into the world from God. One of the great messianic pictures of the time, drawn from the book of Daniel, is that of the '**son of man**', who is exalted to a seat alongside God and given the task of bringing God's judgment to the world. So when Jesus finds the man who had been healed – and who has now been thrown out of the synagogue – and asks him whether he believes in the son of man, this is what he means. Is he prepared to put his trust in the one who has come to bring God's judgment, God's dangerous but healing light, into the world?

The man, not unnaturally, seeks further clarity. Who is this son of man, he asks. (The question continues to echo through the **gospel**, as we find in 12.34.) He has already declared that Jesus is a prophet (9.17). He has stuck to his story, that it was Jesus who opened his eyes (9.25, 30–33). Now he is invited to make the further step: Jesus is not just a prophet, not just a unique healer, but is the one through whom God's light, searing with truth and holiness, is coming into the world. Suddenly the picture comes into complete focus for him, and he believes – one of many individuals, throughout John's story, who make the final step which John wants every reader of his book to make (20.31). So what if they've thrown him out of the synagogue? So what if the authorities, real and self-appointed, have declared him to be 'born in sin from top to toe' (9.34)? He must follow where the truth leads, even if those who were supposed to know the truth are suppressing it.

The position of the man's accusers – the hardline **Pharisees** who are sticking to their principles at the cost of the evidence – is then all the more devastatingly exposed. Not only are they wrong, but they have constructed a system within which they will never see that they are wrong. It is one thing to be genuinely mistaken, and to be open to new evidence, new arguments, new insights. It is another to create a closed world, like a sealed room, into which no light, no fresh air, can come from outside.

Their condition, in fact, is not far removed from that which Paul describes in the first chapter of Romans (1.32). There are some people who not only do the wrong thing but adjust their vision of the moral universe so that they can label evil as 'good' and good as 'evil'. Once that has happened, such people have effectively struck a deal not only with evil but with death itself. They have turned away from the **life**-giving God and locked themselves into a way of thinking and living which systematically excludes him – and, with him, the prospect and possibility of rescue.

So who decides when the picture is in focus? The New Testament gives the central answer: Jesus. As we have seen, Jesus' work will be continued, after his ascension, by the holy spirit. But it's Jesus himself who brings light and truth to the world. The power of lies, and of evil, is very strong. It is easy to be deceived. Only by checking back to Jesus, over and over again, can we be quite sure that we are standing alongside the man born blind, in his new-found **faith** and openness to God's light. The alternative is to stand beside the Pharisees, certain of their rightness, but locked and bolted into a darkness of their own devising.

JOHN 10.1–10

The Good Shepherd

[1]'I'm telling you the solemn truth,' said Jesus. 'Anyone who doesn't come into the sheepfold by the gate, but gets in by some other way, is a thief and a brigand. [2]But the one who comes in through the gate is

104

the sheep's own shepherd. ³The doorkeeper will open up for him, and the sheep hear his voice. He calls his own sheep by name, and leads them out. ⁴When he has brought out all that belong to him, he goes on ahead of them. The sheep follow him, because they know his voice. ⁵They won't follow a stranger; instead, they will run away from him, because they don't know the stranger's voice.'

⁶Jesus spoke this parable to them, but they didn't understand what it was he was saying to them.

⁷So he spoke to them again.

'I'm telling you the solemn truth,' he said. 'I am the gate of the sheep. ⁸All the people who came before me were thieves and brigands, but the sheep didn't listen to them. ⁹I am the gate. If anyone comes in by me, they will be safe, and will go in and out and find pasture. ¹⁰The thief only comes to steal, and kill, and destroy. I came so that they could have life – yes, and have it full to overflowing.'

We stood on the cliffs and watched as the mother birds swooped in from the sea with mouthfuls of fish. There, below us, were thousands, probably tens of thousands, of young birds, all waiting eagerly, all screaming their peculiar cry. They were all jostling and pushing, falling over and scrambling about. Somehow, unerringly, the mothers picked out the single voice of their own chick from the teeming, noisy crowd. It seemed like a **miracle**.

I suppose we shouldn't be too surprised. Perhaps all human voices sound alike to birds – yet a father or mother will recognize their child's voice in a crowded room. But those of us who don't have much to do with the bird and animal kingdoms on a daily basis are often startled at just how much animals can distinguish between different people as well as between other members of their own species. To this day, in the Middle East, a shepherd will go into a crowded sheepfold and call out his own sheep one by one, naming them. They will recognize his voice and come to him.

The shepherd, after all, spends most hours of most days in their company. He knows their individual characters, markings, likes and dislikes. What's more, they know him. They know his voice. Someone else can come to the sheepfold and they won't go near him, even if he calls the right names. They are listening for the one voice that matters, the voice they trust. When they hear it, he won't need a sheepdog to keep them in order. He won't walk behind them, driving them on. He will walk ahead, calling them, and they will follow him. I've seen it done.

The first paragraph of this section (verses 1–5) is a **parable**, as John tells us in verse 6. It's perhaps not surprising that Jesus' hearers didn't understand it. In fact, Jesus adds three layers of explanation: one in the present passage (verses 7–10), another in the next (verses 11–18) and then the last in verses 25–30. We will need each of these to get to the bottom of what he meant. But it's important to read these opening verses as they stand, and hear first what they themselves have to say.

In our Bibles this is the start of what we call 'chapter 10', but when the book was written there weren't any divisions into chapters and verses. We should read this passage remembering what has just been going on. The question that dominated chapter 9 was: is Jesus from God or not? Is he a prophet or not? Is he the **Messiah** or not, the '**son of man**' whom God will set as judge over the world? Now here, in what we call chapter 10, we have a parable about shepherds and sheep. What's the connection?

The answer is that in the Bible the picture of the shepherd with his sheep is frequently used to refer to the king and his people. In the modern world we don't think of rulers and leaders in quite that way. We think of people running big companies, of the presidents of banks and transnational corporations. We think of people sitting behind desks, dictating letters or chairing meetings. Often such people are quite removed from most of those who work in the organization. They seldom see them face to face, and probably don't know the names of very many. But in the Bible the ideal king is pictured as a shepherd (Ezekiel 34), perhaps modelled on the shepherd-boy David, who became the king after God's own heart. In a world where they knew about the intimate contact and trust between shepherd and sheep, this was their preferred way of talking about kingship.

This is the image that Jesus chooses to explain his own claim to be the true king of Israel. Though generations of Bible readers have hurried on to verse 11, where Jesus calls himself 'the good shepherd', we should notice that in these first five verses he doesn't mention himself directly. He is talking, as it were in the abstract, about the difference between true shepherds and false ones.

Who are these false ones, these 'thieves and brigands', these 'strangers'? Jesus almost certainly has in mind the various leaders who had emerged during his own lifetime. Some, whom we might call revolutionary leaders or warlords, were eager to lead Israel into confrontation with the imperial powers. Others, particularly the house of Herod, were eager to submit to Rome as long as that meant keeping their own power and wealth. Jesus is posing the question: how will you tell God's true, appointed king when he comes?

The answer is that you can tell the true king the same way you can tell the true shepherd. Anybody can turn up in Jerusalem and give himself airs as a leader. But only the one who comes by the way God has appointed has the right to do so. Anyone can call followers. But the sign of the real king is the response that comes from the heart, when people hear his voice and, in love and trust, follow him.

The parable of these first five verses, it seems, is designed to say: this is what I'm doing; this is what gives substance to my claim to be sent by God as Israel's true king. The fact that people are hearing me and following me – notably the man born blind – is the sign that God has sent me.

But, faced with blank stares from his audience, Jesus continues with further explanations. The first, in verses 7–10, highlights another part of the shepherd's role. He is the gate, or door. In many Eastern sheepfolds, the shepherd lies down at night in the gateway, to stop the sheep getting out and to stop predators getting in. Here Jesus seems to indicate the way in which the shepherd keeps the sheep safe, and, like God himself in Psalm 121.8, watches over their going out and their coming in. The emphasis is on the safety, and the fulfilled life, of the sheep. The shepherd has no business looking after his own interests. His priority are the sheep. Find a king like that, and you've found the Lord's anointed.

The promise of full **life**, full to overflowing, is as relevant for us today as it was then. The modern Western world has discovered how unsatisfying materialism really is, and is looking for something more, something beyond. Many thieves have told lies, and have deceived the sheep, stolen them and left them for dead. The call today to Jesus' true sheep is to listen for his voice, and to find in him and him alone the life which is overflowing life indeed.

JOHN 10.11–18

The Shepherd and the Sheep

[11]'I am the good shepherd,' Jesus continued. 'The good shepherd lays down his life for the sheep. [12]But supposing there's a hired servant, who isn't himself the shepherd, and who doesn't himself own the sheep. He will see the wolf coming, and leave the sheep, and run away. Then the wolf will snatch the sheep and scatter them. [13]He'll run away because he's only a hired servant, and doesn't care about the sheep.

[14]'I am the good shepherd. I know my own sheep, and my own know me – [15]just as the father knows me and I know the father. And I lay down my life for the sheep. [16]And I have other sheep, too, which don't belong to this sheepfold. I must bring them, too, and they will hear my voice. Then there will be one flock, and one shepherd.

[17]'That's why the father loves me, because I lay down my life, so that I can take it again. [18]Nobody takes it from me; I lay it down of my own accord. I have the right to lay it down, and I have the right to receive it back again. This is the command I received from my father.'

I was talking to a friend who had been in business most of his life.

'The trouble with so many business leaders today', he said, 'is that they're only in it for their own quick profit. Once people were really concerned about making something worthwhile, about building up a business, about looking after their workers. They would hope that their children would carry on the business after them, and go on contributing to the well-being of the local community. Now they don't care. They can close a factory in one town and open another one a hundred miles away. As long as they get their bonus and share options they don't worry about anything else.'

How true that is I can't of course say. No doubt it varies from country to country, and from one company to another. But it leads us towards the point Jesus is making here. The definition of the true shepherd is that he isn't in it for his own profit. In fact, the supreme test of what he's in it for will come when he's faced with a choice. A predator appears – a lion, a wolf or a bear. You can tell the difference between the true shepherd and the false one by what they do. The false shepherd saves his prospects at the cost of his reputation. The true shepherd shows who he is by being prepared to die for the sheep.

This development of the **parable** introduces the dark note which, as John unfolds his whole story, will come to dominate events all too soon. Throughout the last chapters we have seen Jesus facing death threats. Now he declares that violent death is not just a dangerous possibility; it's his vocation. And the best explanation of why this might be so is found, not in heavy volumes of abstract theology, but in this very parable, this very down-to-earth picture of the shepherd and the sheep. The sheep are facing danger; the shepherd will go to meet it, and, if necessary, he will take upon himself the fate that would otherwise befall the sheep. In Jesus' case, it was necessary, and he did.

The strange thing about this is that despite the apparent gloom of this vocation – what use, after all, is a dead shepherd? – Jesus also speaks of the grand prospect that lies before him in another part of the same calling. He isn't going to rest content with delivering the present sheep from the danger they face. He is going to enlarge the flock considerably by bringing in a whole lot of very different sheep (verse 16). What is he talking about?

The original 'sheep' are the people of Israel. Jesus is calling them, and those from among his Jewish contemporaries who are ready for the call are hearing his voice, trusting him and coming to him. But, as Israel's prophets and wise writers had always hinted, the God of Israel was never interested *only* in Israel. His call to Israel was for the sake of the whole world. The 'other sheep' are that great company, from every nation under **heaven**, that God intends to save, and to save through Jesus. The Jewish **Messiah** is to become the Lord, the shepherd, of the whole world.

This theme, too, will grow and swell in the coming chapters. When Jesus eventually faces Pontius Pilate, the official representative of the ruling pagan power, he is looking at someone who, though not himself a Jew, is a potential 'sheep', to be challenged with a vision of God's **kingdom** and truth (18.33–38). The **Gentiles** are no longer the enemy. They are sheep who have not yet been brought into the sheepfold. Take a moment to think through how this announcement must have sounded in a world – Jesus' own world – filled with hatred and suspicion, with violence and counter-violence.

Everything is based on, and returns into, that close and intimate relationship which Jesus had with 'the father', and which so much of this **gospel** has already explored. The father loves the shepherd, especially because he will express the father's own love for the world by giving up his life for it. If he does this in obedience to the father's will, he will also receive it back again (verse 18); Jesus here makes the Jewish hope of general **resurrection** the personal and specific aim of his own work, anticipating the longer discussion in the next chapter. And the bond of trust and love which ties together the shepherd and the sheep is the same bond that links father and son. This, too, will be developed further in a later chapter (chapter 17).

Behind this, all through, is the ancient prophecy in Ezekiel 34. There's a strange thing in that chapter. Sometimes the prophet speaks of God becoming the true shepherd of Israel. But then, later, he speaks of David – in other words, of the Messiah – as the true shepherd, with God being God over shepherd and sheep alike. 'Well, which is it?' we want to ask Ezekiel. 'Is God the shepherd, or is the Messiah the shepherd?' He doesn't answer. He just points into the future. Only in this tenth chapter of John do we see how it all fits together. As Jesus will finally say in verse 30, 'I and the father are one.' God is the shepherd; the king is the shepherd. It makes sense in Jesus, and nowhere else.

All this should make it clear why Jesus refers to himself as the '*good*' shepherd (verses 11 and 14). But our word 'good' doesn't quite catch the full meaning of the word John has written here. For us, 'good' can sound a bit cold or hard, merely moralistic. The word John uses can also mean 'beautiful'. This doesn't refer to what Jesus looked like. It's about the sheer attractiveness of what, as the shepherd, he was doing. When he calls, people want to come. When they realize he has died for them, they want to even more. The point of calling Jesus 'the good shepherd' is to emphasize the strange, compelling power of his love.

JOHN 10.19-30

The Messiah and the Father

¹⁹So there was again a division among the Judaeans because of what Jesus had said.

²⁰'He's demon-possessed!' some were saying. 'He's raving mad! Why listen to him?'

²¹'No,' said some others, 'that's not how demon-possessed people talk. Anyway, how could a demon open a blind man's eyes?'

²²It was the Feast of the Dedication in Jerusalem. It was winter, ²³and Jesus was walking in the Temple, in Solomon's Porch. ²⁴The Judaeans surrounded him.

'How much longer are you going to keep us in suspense?' they asked. 'If you are the Messiah, say so out loud!'

²⁵'I told you,' replied Jesus, 'and you didn't believe. The works which I'm doing in my father's name give evidence about me. ²⁶But you don't believe, because you don't belong to my sheep.

²⁷'My sheep hear my voice. I know them, and they follow me. ²⁸I give them the life of the coming age. They will never, ever perish, and nobody can snatch them out of my hand. ²⁹My father, who has given them to me, is greater than all, and nobody can snatch them out of my father's hand. ³⁰I and the father are one.'

It was the third winter after the disaster. Many of the people had begun to lose hope that good fortune would ever return to them. The enemy had come in and trampled all over their lovely city. Many had been killed, many captured. Some of the local people had collaborated with the foreigners, hoping no doubt to secure their favour in case their regime should last a long time.

But some had never reconciled themselves to the new situation. In particular, the loss of their great and beautiful **Temple** was a shock and an affront. It was, after all, the house of their God, the God of all the world. Now these foreigners were worshipping their own gods there, offering **sacrifices** that would never have been allowed before. Revolution was brewing, and came to the boil. A sudden attack, a wonderful victory; the tyrant was overthrown, the city liberated.

Three years to the day after the disaster, they solemnly purified the Temple. The offered the proper sacrifices, they lit the lamps, and they prayed to the God of **heaven** and earth that they might never suffer such a thing again. And they commanded that every year a festival should be kept to commemorate the occasion. It is called Hanukkah, 'dedication', and it falls on the 25th day of the Jewish month Chislev, roughly the equivalent of our December.

The year was 167 BC; the tyrant was Antiochus Epiphanes; the hero of the resistance was Judas Maccabaeus. And the significant thing for our purposes was that through this remarkable act of courage and religious devotion, Judas and his family became kings. To liberate the Temple from the enemy, and to reconsecrate it, was as close as you could come to doing again what David and Solomon had done. So, even though Judas wasn't a descendant of David, he started a dynasty which lasted for a hundred years. When it ended, the Romans made Herod the Great king instead – and he married a princess from the family of Judas Maccabaeus, to show he intended to continue the line.

So every time the Jewish people celebrated Hanukkah, they not only thought about God and liberation. They not only thanked God for having the Temple back again. They also thought about kings, and how they became kings. And here is Jesus, walking in the Temple during the festival of Hanukkah, talking about the good shepherd, the real shepherd, the king who would come and show all the others up as a bunch of thieves and brigands. Never let it be thought that Jesus' **message** was anything other than controversial – and dangerous. Never forget that the famous 'good shepherd' chapter ends up with people trying to stone Jesus to death.

Controversy and danger are certainly in the air in this passage. Often when we think of Jesus as the 'good shepherd' we imagine pictures of him with flowers in his hair, surrounded by happy children, with a few sheep as well to give the picture a pastoral touch. I remember such pictures from my childhood. The reality – the real question he was talking about when he spoke of himself as the good shepherd – was and is very different. It was and is all about power and rule, about God's **kingdom** and the world's kingdoms, about God appointing a true king, not where there had been a vacuum waiting for someone to fill it, but where there had been too many kings, too many rulers, and all of them anxious and ready to strike out at anyone trying to stake a new claim.

Once again the cry goes up, as often in the **gospels**: this man must be **demon**-possessed! This was, after all, almost the only thing you could say if you'd seen what he was doing, heard what he was saying, and yet were determined not to believe that the living God was uniquely at work in him. But this time, unlike the other times when the accusation is made, it isn't Jesus who replies, but some in the crowd – some of the sheep, Jesus might have said, who have already heard his voice and found themselves following him. They know that what he's done simply isn't the sort of thing that demon-possessed people do. Demons are into destruction, not into extraordinary acts of rescue and healing.

But then, as so often in John, we come back to the double question which haunts the gospel story. Is Jesus then the **Messiah**, Israel's true king? Jesus will not say it in so many words, though anyone listening closely to what he'd said about the good shepherd would have picked up the message easily enough. (That is presumably why he says that he told them and they didn't believe.) As usual, he refers them instead to the works that he's doing. If they can't draw the right conclusion from what he's done, adding more words won't do any good.

But the discussion doesn't stop there. Jesus presses on into even more dangerous territory. He returns once more to the shepherd-and-sheep theme, this time with a glorious and spectacular promise to the 'sheep'. Those who hear Jesus' voice and recognize it as the voice of 'their' shepherd will be safe for ever. He will look after them, and even death itself, the last great enemy, cannot ultimately harm them. The reason Jesus can be so confident of this is that the guarantee is his own unbreakable bond of love and union with the father, and the fact that the 'sheep' he owns are the ones the father has given him.

Christian confidence about the future beyond death, in other words, is not a matter of wishful thinking, a vague general hope, or a temperamental inclination to assume things will turn out all right. It is built firmly on nothing less than the union of Jesus with the father – one of the main themes of this whole gospel. It is interesting to observe that where, in Christian thinking, people have become unclear on Jesus' close relation to the father, they have often become unclear also on the certainty of Christian hope, and vice versa.

JOHN 10.31-42

Blasphemy!

[31]So the Judaeans once more picked up stones to stone him.

[32]'I've shown you many fine deeds from the father,' Jesus replied to them. 'Which of these deeds are you stoning me for?'

[33]'We're not stoning you for good deeds,' replied the Judaeans, 'but because of blasphemy! Here you are, a mere man, and you're making yourself into God!'

[34]'It's written in your law, isn't it,' replied Jesus to them, '"I said, you are gods?" [35]Well, if the law calls people "gods", people to whom God's word came (and you can't set the Bible aside), [36]how can you accuse someone of blasphemy when the father has placed him apart and sent him into the world, and he says, "I am the son of God"?

[37]'If I'm not doing the works of my father, don't believe me. [38]But if I am doing them, well – even if you don't believe me, believe the

works! That way you will know and grasp that the father is in me, and I am in the father.'

³⁹So again they tried to arrest him. But Jesus managed to get away from them.

⁴⁰He went off once more across the Jordan, to the place where John had been baptizing at the beginning, and he stayed there. ⁴¹Several people came to him.

'John never did any signs,' they said, 'but everything that John said about this man was true.'

⁴²And many believed in him there.

They found the music, a single manuscript copy, among the piles of unsorted paper the composer had left at the time of his death. It was clearly a piece for solo violin, but it looked extraordinary: difficult, daring, probably unplayable. Above it was scrawled, in his shaky hand: To the City Guild of Violinists.

The City Guild was honoured, but embarrassed. None of them could play the piece. Copies were made, and each member took one home to try it out. When they met later they tried to pass it off with excuses. Surely the old man couldn't have meant you to play *those* notes simultaneously? His mind must have been wandering. Anyway, it seemed very strange – not much tune to it, though they couldn't deny there were interesting passages. All of them declared that they'd give it another try . . . one day. Some even wondered aloud whether the old man hadn't meant it to be played at all – it was just a strange and impossible idea. And they all quietly forgot about it.

Until one day, many years later, there came to the city an old man with a long straggly beard and a battered violin case. He hardly looked like a real musician: a gypsy, people thought, or a travelling tradesman with a second line in music teaching. He took lodgings just by the main city square. Not long afterwards, rumours began to circulate of strange and beautiful music being heard after dark. Finally some of the City Guild gathered under the windows.

There was no mistaking it. They were listening to the music that had been dedicated to them. It was, indeed, almost unplayable; almost, but not quite. He was playing it, making it dance and leap and swell and fall. It was wild and strange and headstrong and sweet.

As it died away, some of the City Guild burst into spontaneous applause. But others were furious. 'That was *our* music,' they said. 'He's not a member of the Guild! What right has he got to come here and play it? Trying to make us look stupid!'

The window opened, and the old man looked out.

'I'm his son,' he said. 'He taught me to play the piece. And he made me a member of the Guild before he died. He was its honorary President, you know.'

'Rubbish!' shouted the angry violinists in the square below. 'You've no business here! How dare you!'

The next morning the violinist had gone. The music was never heard in the city again.

In this passage, Jesus quotes a biblical verse that has puzzled many people. It comes from Psalm 82. God himself is speaking, addressing a group of people, and warning them that, although they claim to have a special status, they haven't lived up to it. They had some music given to them, but they couldn't play it.

The status in question, to our surprise – granted that the Jews believed there was only one God – is that they are themselves 'gods':

I said, you are gods,
    and all of you children of the Most High;
Still, you will die like humans,
    and fall like any old princeling.

In Jesus' day, some learned Jewish thinkers reckoned that the psalm was talking about the children of Israel at Mount Sinai. When God gave them the **law**, it was like a master composer leaving a piece of music for the local musicians to play. Had they but known it, they were made noble, even divine, simply by receiving it; when the law arrived, mere possession of it exalted Israel to superhuman status. It was God's own **word** and will. But, though some Israelites struggled hard to keep the law, they failed dismally. Aaron made the golden calf at the foot of Mount Sinai, and after that things never really got much better. They broke the law again and again. According to unanimous Jewish thinking, that was why they went into **exile** in Babylon.

But the memory remained, through Psalm 82, of what might have been. 'I said, "you are gods".'

And now there arrives in town someone who isn't even part of the regular guild of law students, and he begins to do things which cause people to make strange claims about him. It's as though he's playing the music for the first time; and they're horrified, because they didn't know anyone could do it, and it had become almost an article of **faith** with them that nobody *could* do it. 'I said, you are gods,' he quotes back at them; 'so why are you bothered about what you hear me saying?'

The implication is staggering. The union of humanity and divinity which has arrived in their midst – the wild, strange, headstrong and

114

sweet song of incarnation – is not, after all, a bizarre or impossible thing. It is as though the composer knew all along that his son would one day come and play the music – and that, if it was to be appreciated, others had first to try it and fail. They wouldn't like it, but that too would be part of the plan, part of the music. But in the midst of it the son would be saying to them 'Don't you see? The father is present in me, and I in the father . . .'

Once again, the onlookers are bidden to think about the works Jesus had done – the 'signs', as he says in verse 41 – and draw the appropriate conclusion. How could he play this music, full of healing and new creation, in this way? Only because he and the father really were bound together in a wonderful unity that shocked and startled them then, and that still shocks and startles people in various cultures today.

But if the Guild of Official Religious Persons in Jerusalem had difficulty with Jesus' claim, even the country-folk in the land beyond the Jordan could draw the right conclusions. They, after all, had nothing to lose. They knew what **John the Baptist** had said about Jesus, and they could see that it was coming true. The question we have to face today is whether we are ready to look at Jesus with that open, vulnerable gaze, and to draw the right conclusion for ourselves. Only so will we hear the music once more.

GLOSSARY

the accuser, *see* the satan

age to come, *see* present age

apostle, disciple, the Twelve
'Apostle' means 'one who is sent'. It could be used of an ambassador or official delegate. In the New Testament it is sometimes used specifically of Jesus' inner circle of twelve; but Paul sees not only himself but several others outside the Twelve as 'apostles', the criterion being whether the person had personally seen the risen Jesus. Jesus' own choice of twelve close associates symbolized his plan to renew God's people, Israel; after the death of Judas Iscariot (Matthew 27.5; Acts 1.18), Matthias was chosen by lot to take his place, preserving the symbolic meaning. During Jesus' lifetime they, and many other followers, were seen as his 'disciples', which means 'pupils' or 'apprentices'.

baptism
Literally, 'plunging' people into water. From within a wider Jewish tradition of ritual washings and bathings, **John the Baptist** undertook a vocation of baptizing people in the Jordan, not as one ritual among others but as a unique moment of **repentance**, preparing them for the coming of the **kingdom of God**. Jesus himself was baptized by John, identifying himself with this renewal movement and developing it in his own way. His followers in turn baptized others. After his **resurrection**, and the sending of the **holy spirit**, baptism became the normal sign and means of entry into the community of Jesus' people. As early as Paul it was aligned both with the **Exodus** from Egypt (1 Corinthians 10.2) and with Jesus' death and resurrection (Romans 6.2–11).

Christ, *see* Messiah

circumcision, circumcised
The cutting off of the foreskin. Male circumcision was a major mark of identity for Jews, following its initial commandment to Abraham (Genesis 17), reinforced by Joshua (Joshua 5.2–9). Other peoples, e.g. the Egyptians, also circumcised male children. A line of thought from Deuteronomy (e.g. 30.6), through Jeremiah (e.g. 31.33), to the **Dead Sea Scrolls** and the New Testament (e.g. Romans 2.29) speaks of 'circumcision of the heart' as God's real desire, by which one may become inwardly what the male Jew is outwardly, that is, marked out as part

of God's people. At periods of Jewish assimilation into the surrounding culture, some Jews tried to remove the marks of circumcision (e.g. 1 Maccabees 1.11–15).

covenant
At the heart of Jewish belief is the conviction that the one God, YHWH, who had made the whole world, had called Abraham and his family to belong to him in a special way. The promises God made to Abraham and his family, and the requirements that were laid on them as a result, came to be seen in terms either of the agreement that a king would make with a subject people, or sometimes of the marriage bond between husband and wife. One regular way of describing this relationship was 'covenant', which can thus include both promise and **law**. The covenant was renewed at Mount Sinai with the giving of the **Torah**; in Deuteronomy before the entry to the promised land; and, in a more focused way, with David (e.g. Psalm 89). Jeremiah 31 promised that after the punishment of **exile** God would make a 'new covenant' with his people, forgiving them and binding them to him more intimately. Jesus believed that this was coming true through his **kingdom** proclamation and his death and **resurrection**. The early Christians developed these ideas in various ways, believing that in Jesus the promises had at last been fulfilled.

Dead Sea Scrolls
A collection of texts, some in remarkably good repair, some extremely fragmentary, found in the late 1940s around Qumran (near the north-east corner of the Dead Sea), and virtually all now edited, translated and in the public domain. They formed all or part of the library of a strict monastic group, most likely Essenes, founded in the mid-second century BC and lasting until the Jewish–Roman war of 66–70. The scrolls include the earliest existing manuscripts of the Hebrew and Aramaic scriptures, and several other important documents of community regulations, scriptural exegesis, hymns, wisdom writings, and other literature. They shed a flood of light on one small segment within the Judaism of Jesus' day, helping us to understand how some Jews at least were thinking, praying and reading scripture. Despite attempts to prove the contrary, they make no reference to **John the Baptist**, Jesus, Paul, James or early Christianity in general.

demons, *see* the satan

devil, *see* the satan

disciple, *see* apostle

Essenes, *see* Dead Sea Scrolls

eucharist
The meal in which the earliest Christians, and Christians ever since, obeyed Jesus' command to 'do this in remembrance of him' at the Last Supper (Luke

22.19; 1 Corinthians 11.23–26). The word 'eucharist' itself comes from the Greek for 'thanksgiving'; it means, basically, 'the thank-you meal', and looks back to the many times when Jesus took bread, gave thanks for it, broke it and gave it to people (e.g. Luke 24.30; John 6.11). Other early phrases for the same meal are 'the Lord's Supper' (1 Corinthians 11.20) and 'the breaking of bread' (Acts 2.42). Later it came to be called 'the mass' (from the Latin word at the end of the service, meaning 'sent out') and 'holy communion' (Paul speaks of 'sharing' or 'communion' in the body and blood of Christ). Later theological controversies about the precise meaning of the various actions and elements of the meal should not obscure its centrality in earliest Christian living and its continuing vital importance today.

exile

Deuteronomy (29–30) warned that if Israel disobeyed YHWH, he would send his people into exile, but that if they then repented he would bring them back. When the Babylonians sacked Jerusalem and took the people into exile, prophets such as Jeremiah interpreted this as the fulfilment of this prophecy, and made further promises about how long exile would last (70 years, according to Jeremiah 25.12; 29.10). Sure enough, exiles began to return in the late sixth century (Ezra 1.1). However, the post-exilic period was largely a disappointment, since the people were still enslaved to foreigners (Nehemiah 9.36); and at the height of persecution by the Syrians, Daniel 9.2, 24 spoke of the 'real' exile lasting not for 70 years but for 70 *weeks* of years, i.e., 490 years. Longing for the real 'return from exile', when the prophecies of Isaiah, Jeremiah, etc. would be fulfilled, and redemption from pagan oppression accomplished, continued to characterize many Jewish movements, and was a major theme in Jesus' proclamation and his summons to **repentance**.

Exodus

The Exodus from Egypt took place, according to the book of that name, under the leadership of Moses, after long years in which the Israelites had been enslaved there. (According to Genesis 15.13f., this was itself part of God's covenanted promise to Abraham.) It demonstrated, to them and to Pharaoh, King of Egypt, that Israel was God's special child (Exodus 4.22). They then wandered through the Sinai wilderness for 40 years, led by God in a pillar of cloud and fire; early on in this time they were given the **Torah** on Mount Sinai itself. Finally, after the death of Moses and under the leadership of Joshua, they crossed the Jordan and entered, and eventually conquered, the promised land of Canaan. This event, commemorated annually in Passover and other Jewish festivals, gave the Israelites not only a powerful memory of what had made them a people, but also a particular shape and content to their faith in YHWH as not only creator but also redeemer; and in subsequent enslavements, particularly the **exile**, they looked for a further redemption which would be, in effect, a new Exodus. Probably no other past event so dominated the imagination of first-century Jews;

119

among them the early Christians, following the lead of Jesus himself, continually referred back to the Exodus to give meaning and shape to their own critical events, most particularly Jesus' death and **resurrection**.

faith

Faith in the New Testament covers a wide area of human trust and trustworthiness, merging into love at one end of the scale and loyalty at the other. Within Jewish and Christian thinking faith in God also includes *belief*, accepting certain things as true about God, and what he has done in the world (e.g. bringing Israel out of Egypt; raising Jesus from the dead). For Jesus, 'faith' often seems to mean 'recognizing that God is decisively at work to bring the **kingdom** through Jesus'. For Paul, 'faith' is both the specific belief that Jesus is Lord and that God raised him from the dead (Romans 10.9) and the response of grateful human love to sovereign divine love (Galatians 2.20). This faith is, for Paul, the solitary badge of membership in God's people in **Christ**, marking them out in a way that **Torah**, and the works it prescribes, can never do.

Gentiles

The Jews divided the world into Jews and non-Jews. The Hebrew word for non-Jews, *goyim*, carries overtones both of family identity (i.e., not of Jewish ancestry) and of worship (i.e., of idols, not of the one true God YHWH). Though many Jews established good relations with Gentiles, not least in the Jewish Diaspora (the dispersion of Jews away from Palestine), officially there were taboos against contact such as intermarriage. In the New Testament the Greek word *ethne*, 'nations', carries the same meanings as *goyim*. Part of Paul's overmastering agenda was to insist that Gentiles who believed in Jesus had full rights in the Christian community alongside believing Jews, without having to become **circumcised**.

good news, gospel, message, word

The idea of 'good news', for which an older English word is 'gospel', had two principal meanings for first-century Jews. First, with roots in Isaiah, it meant the news of YHWH's long-awaited victory over evil and rescue of his people. Second, it was used in the Roman world of the accession, or birthday, of the emperor. Since for Jesus and Paul the announcement of God's inbreaking **kingdom** was both the fulfilment of prophecy and a challenge to the world's present rulers, 'gospel' became an important shorthand for both the message of Jesus himself, and the apostolic message about him. Paul saw this message as itself the vehicle of God's saving power (Romans 1.16; 1 Thessalonians 2.13).

The four canonical 'gospels' tell the story of Jesus in such a way as to bring out both these aspects (unlike some other so-called 'gospels' circulated in the second and subsequent centuries, which tended both to cut off the scriptural and Jewish roots of Jesus' achievement and to inculcate a private spirituality rather than confrontation with the world's rulers). Since in Isaiah this creative, life-giving good news was seen as God's own powerful word (40.8; 55.11), the early Christians could use 'word' or 'message' as another shorthand for the basic Christian proclamation.

gospel, *see* **good news**

heaven

Heaven is God's dimension of the created order (Genesis 1.1; Psalm 115.16; Matthew 6.9), whereas 'earth' is the world of space, time and matter that we know. 'Heaven' thus sometimes stands, reverentially, for 'God' (as in Matthew's regular '**kingdom of heaven**'). Normally hidden from human sight, heaven is occasionally revealed or unveiled so that people can see God's dimension of ordinary life (e.g. 2 Kings 6.17; Revelation 1, 4—5). Heaven in the New Testament is thus not usually seen as the place where God's people go after death; at the end the New Jerusalem descends *from* heaven *to* earth, joining the two dimensions for ever. 'Entering the kingdom of heaven' does not mean 'going to heaven after death', but belonging in the present to the people who steer their earthly course by the standards and purposes of heaven (cf. the Lord's Prayer: 'on earth as in heaven', Matthew 6. 10) and who are assured of membership in the **age to come.**

Herodians

Herod the Great ruled Judaea from 37 to 4 BC; after his death his territory was divided between his sons Archelaus, Herod Antipas (the Herod of the **gospels**), and Philip. The Herodians supported the claims of Antipas to be the true king of the Jews. Though the **Pharisees** would normally oppose such a claim, they could make common cause with the Herodians when facing a common threat (e.g. Jesus, Mark 3.6).

high priest, *see* **priests**

holy spirit

In Genesis 1.2, the spirit is God's presence and power *within* creation, without God being identified with creation. The same spirit entered people, notably the prophets, enabling them to speak and act for God. At his **baptism** by **John the Baptist,** Jesus was specially equipped with the spirit, resulting in his remarkable public career (Acts 10.38). After his **resurrection,** his followers were themselves filled (Acts 2) by the same spirit, now identified as Jesus' own spirit: the creator God was acting afresh, remaking the world and them too. The spirit enabled them to live out a holiness which the **Torah** could not, producing 'fruit' in their lives, giving them 'gifts' with which to serve God, the world and the church, and assuring them of future resurrection (Romans 8; Galatians 4—5; 1 Corinthians 12—14). From very early in Christianity (e.g. Galatians 4.1-7), the spirit became part of the new revolutionary definition of God himself: 'the one who sends the son and the spirit of the son'.

John (the Baptist)

Jesus' cousin on his mother's side, born a few months before Jesus; his father was a **priest**. He acted as a prophet, baptizing in the Jordan – dramatically re-enacting the **Exodus** from Egypt – to prepare people, by **repentance**, for God's coming judgment. He may have had some contact with the **Essenes**, though his eventual public message was different from theirs. Jesus' own vocation was decisively confirmed at his **baptism** by John. As part of John's message of the **kingdom**, he outspokenly criticized Herod Antipas for marrying his brother's wife. Herod had him imprisoned, and then beheaded him at his wife's request (Mark 6.14–29). Groups of John's disciples continued a separate existence, without merging into Christianity, for some time afterwards (e.g. Acts 19.1–7).

justification

God's declaration, from his position as judge of all the world, that someone is in the right, despite universal sin. This declaration will be made on the last day on the basis of an entire life (Romans 2.1–16), but is brought forward into the present on the basis of Jesus' achievement, because sin has been dealt with through his cross (Romans 3.21—4.25); the means of this present justification is simply **faith**. This means, particularly, that Jews and **Gentiles** alike are full members of the family promised by God to Abraham (Galatians 3; Romans 4).

kingdom of God, kingdom of heaven

Best understood as the king*ship*, or sovereign and saving rule, of Israel's God YHWH, as celebrated in several psalms (e.g. 99.1) and prophecies (e.g. Daniel 6.26f.). Because YHWH was the creator God, when he finally became king in the way he intended this would involve setting the world to rights, and particularly rescuing Israel from its enemies. 'Kingdom of God' and various equivalents (e.g. 'No king but God!') became a revolutionary slogan around the time of Jesus. Jesus' own announcement of God's kingdom redefined these expectations around his own very different plan and vocation. His invitation to people to 'enter' the kingdom was a way of summoning them to allegiance to himself and his programme, seen as the start of God's long-awaited saving reign. For Jesus, the kingdom was coming not in a single move, but in stages, of which his own public career was one, his death and **resurrection** another, and a still future consummation another. Note that 'kingdom of **heaven**' is Matthew's preferred form for the same phrase, following a regular Jewish practice of saying 'heaven' rather than 'God'. It does not refer to a place ('heaven'), but to the fact of God's becoming king in and through Jesus and his achievement. Paul speaks of Jesus, as **Messiah**, already in possession of his kingdom, waiting to hand it over finally to the father (1 Corinthians 15.23–28; cf. Ephesians 5.5).

law, *see* Torah

lawyers, legal experts, *see* Pharisees

leper, leprosy

In a world without modern medicine, tight medical controls were needed to prevent the spread of contagious diseases. Several such conditions, mostly severe skin problems, were referred to as 'leprosy', and two long biblical chapters (Leviticus 13—14) are devoted to diagnosis and prevention of it. Sufferers had to live away from towns and shout 'unclean' to warn others not to approach them (13.45). If they were healed, this had to be certified by a priest (14.2–32).

life, soul, spirit

Ancient people held many different views about what made human beings the special creatures they are. Some, including many Jews, believed that to be complete, humans needed bodies as well as inner selves. Others, including many influenced by the philosophy of Plato (fourth century BC), believed that the important part of a human was the 'soul' (Gk: *psyche*), which at death would be happily freed from its bodily prison. Confusingly for us, the same word *psyche* is often used in the New Testament within a Jewish framework where it clearly means 'life' or 'true self', without implying a body/soul dualism that devalues the body. Human inwardness of experience and understanding can also be referred to as 'spirit'. *See also* **resurrection**.

the life of God's coming age, *see* present age

message, *see* good news

Messiah, messianic, Christ

The Hebrew word means literally 'anointed one', hence in theory either a prophet, priest or king. In Greek this translates as *Christos*; 'Christ' in early Christianity was a title, and only gradually became an alternative proper name for Jesus. In practice 'Messiah' is mostly restricted to the notion, which took various forms in ancient Judaism, of the coming king who would be David's true heir, through whom YHWH would bring judgment to the world, and in particular would rescue Israel from pagan enemies. There was no single template of expectations. Scriptural stories and promises contributed to different ideals and movements, often focused on (a) decisive military defeat of Israel's enemies and (b) rebuilding or cleansing the **Temple**. The **Dead Sea Scrolls** speak of two 'Messiahs', one a priest and the other a king. The universal early Christian belief that Jesus was Messiah is only explicable, granted his crucifixion by the Romans (which would have been seen as a clear sign that he was not the Messiah), by their belief that God had raised him from the dead, so vindicating the implicit messianic claims of his earlier ministry.

miracles

Like some of the old prophets, notably Elijah and Elisha, Jesus performed many deeds of remarkable power, particularly healings. The **gospels** refer to these as 'deeds of power', 'signs', 'marvels' or 'paradoxes'. Our word 'miracle' tends to imply that God, normally 'outside' the closed system of the world, sometimes 'intervenes'; miracles have then frequently been denied as a matter of principle. However, in the Bible God is always present, however strangely, and 'deeds of power' are seen as *special* acts of a *present* God rather than as *intrusive* acts of an *absent* one. Jesus' own 'mighty works' are seen particularly, following prophecy, as evidence of his messiahship (e.g. Matthew 11.2–6).

Mishnah

The main codification of Jewish law (**Torah**) by the **rabbis**, produced in about AD 200, reducing to writing the 'oral Torah' which in Jesus' day ran parallel to the 'written Torah'. The Mishnah is itself the basis of the much larger collections of traditions in the two Talmuds (roughly AD 400).

parables

From the Old Testament onwards, prophets and other teachers used various storytelling devices as vehicles for their challenge to Israel (e.g. 2 Samuel 12.1–7). Sometimes these appeared as visions with interpretations (e.g. Daniel 7). Similar techniques were used by the **rabbis**. Jesus made his own creative adaptation of these traditions, in order to break open the world-view of his contemporaries and to invite them to share his vision of God's **kingdom** instead. His stories portrayed this as something that was *happening*, not just a timeless truth, and enabled his hearers to step inside the story and make it their own. As with some Old Testament visions, some of Jesus' parables have their own interpretations (e.g. the sower, Mark 4); others are thinly disguised retellings of the prophetic story of Israel (e.g. the wicked tenants, Mark 12).

parousia

Literally, it means 'presence', as opposed to 'absence', and is sometimes used by Paul with this sense (e.g. Philippians 2.12). It was already used in the Roman world for the ceremonial arrival of, for example, the emperor at a subject city or colony. Although the ascended Lord is not 'absent' from the church, when he 'appears' (Colossians 3.4; 1 John 3.2) in his 'second coming' this will be, in effect, an 'arrival' like that of the emperor, and Paul uses it thus in 1 Corinthians 15.23; 1 Thessalonians 2.19; etc. In the **gospels** it is found only in Matthew 24 (verses 3, 27, 39).

Pharisees, lawyers, legal experts, rabbis

The Pharisees were an unofficial but powerful Jewish pressure group through most of the first centuries BC and AD. Largely lay-led, though including some **priests**, their aim was to purify Israel through intensified observance of the Jewish law (**Torah**), developing their own traditions about the precise meaning and application of scripture, their own patterns of prayer and other devotion, and their own calculations of the national hope. Though not all legal experts were Pharisees, most Pharisees were thus legal experts.

They effected a democratization of Israel's life, since for them the study and practice of Torah was equivalent to worshipping in the **Temple** – though they were adamant in pressing their own rules for the Temple liturgy on an unwilling (and often **Sadducean**) priesthood. This enabled them to survive AD 70 and, merging into the early rabbinic movement, to develop new ways forward. Politically they stood up for ancestral traditions, and were at the forefront of various movements of revolt against both pagan overlordship and compromised Jewish leaders. By Jesus' day there were two distinct schools, the stricter one of Shammai, more inclined towards armed revolt, and the more lenient one of Hillel, ready to live and let live.

Jesus' debates with the Pharisees are at least as much a matter of agenda and policy (Jesus strongly opposed their separatist nationalism) as about details of theology and piety. Saul of Tarsus was a fervent right-wing Pharisee, presumably a Shammaite, until his conversion.

After the disastrous war of AD 66–70, these schools of Hillel and Shammai continued bitter debate on appropriate policy. Following the further disaster of AD 135 (the failed Bar-Kochba revolt against Rome) their traditions were carried on by the rabbis who, though looking to the earlier Pharisees for inspiration, developed a Torah-piety in which personal holiness and purity took the place of political agendas.

present age, age to come, the life of God's coming age

By the time of Jesus many Jewish thinkers divided history into two periods: 'the present age' and 'the age to come' – the latter being the time when YHWH would at last act decisively to judge evil, to rescue Israel, and to create a new world of justice and peace. The early Christians believed that, though the full blessings of the coming age lay still in the future, it had already begun with Jesus, particularly with his death and **resurrection**, and that by **faith** and **baptism** they were able to enter it already. For this reason, the customary translation 'eternal life' is rendered here as 'the life of God's coming age'.

priests, high priest

Aaron, the older brother of Moses, was appointed Israel's first high priest (Exodus 28—29), and in theory his descendants were Israel's priests thereafter. Other members of his tribe (Levi) were 'Levites', performing other liturgical duties but not sacrificing. Priests lived among the people all around the country, having a local teaching role (Leviticus 10.11; Malachi 2.7), and going to Jerusalem by rotation to perform the **Temple** liturgy (e.g. Luke 2.8).

David appointed Zadok (whose Aaronic ancestry is sometimes questioned) as high priest, and his family remained thereafter the senior priests in Jerusalem, probably the ancestors of the **Sadducees**. One explanation of the origins of the **Qumran** Essenes is that they were a dissident group who believed themselves to be the rightful chief priests.

Qumran, *see* **Dead Sea Scrolls**

rabbis, *see* **Pharisees**

repentance

Literally, this means 'turning back'. It is widely used in the Old Testament and subsequent Jewish literature to indicate both a personal turning away from sin and Israel's corporate turning away from idolatry and back to YHWH. Through both meanings, it is linked to the idea of 'return from **exile**'; if Israel is to 'return' in all senses, it must 'return' to YHWH. This is at the heart of the summons of both **John the Baptist** and Jesus. In Paul's writings it is mostly used for **Gentiles** turning away from idols to serve the true God; also for sinning Christians who need to return to Jesus.

resurrection

In most biblical thought, human bodies matter and are not merely disposable prisons for the **soul**. When ancient Israelites wrestled with the goodness and justice of YHWH, the creator, they ultimately came to insist that he must raise the dead (Isaiah 26.19; Daniel 12.2–3) – a suggestion firmly resisted by classical pagan thought. The longed-for return from **exile** was also spoken of in terms of YHWH raising dry bones to new **life** (Ezekiel 37.1–14). These ideas were developed in the second-**Temple** period, not least at times of martyrdom (e.g. 2 Maccabees 7). Resurrection was not just 'life after death', but a newly embodied life *after* 'life after death'; those at present dead were either 'asleep', or seen as 'souls', 'angels' or 'spirits', awaiting new embodiment.

The early Christian belief that Jesus had been raised from the dead was not that he had 'gone to **heaven**', or that he had been 'exalted', or was 'divine'; they believed all those as well, but each could have been expressed without mention of resurrection. Only the bodily resurrection of Jesus explains the rise of the early church, particularly its belief in Jesus' messiahship (which his crucifixion would have called into question). The early Christians believed that they themselves would be raised to a new, transformed bodily life at the time of the Lord's return or **parousia** (e.g. Philippians 3.20f.).

sabbath

The Jewish sabbath, the seventh day of the week, was a regular reminder both of creation (Genesis 2.3; Exodus 20.8–11) and of the **Exodus** (Deuteronomy 5.15). Along with **circumcision** and the food laws, it was one of the badges of Jewish identity within the pagan world of late antiquity, and a considerable body of Jewish **law** and custom grew up around its observance.

sacrifice

Like all ancient people, the Israelites offered animal and vegetable sacrifices to their God. Unlike others, they possessed a highly detailed written code (mostly in Leviticus) for what to offer and how to offer it; this in turn was developed in the **Mishnah** (*c.* AD 200). The Old Testament specifies that sacrifices can only be offered in the Jerusalem **Temple**; after this was destroyed in AD 70, sacrifices ceased, and Judaism developed further the idea, already present in some teachings, of prayer, fasting and almsgiving as alternative forms of sacrifice. The early Christians used the language of sacrifice in connection with such things as holiness, evangelism and the **eucharist**.

Sadducees

By Jesus' day, the Sadducees were the aristocracy of Judaism, possibly tracing their origins to the family of Zadok, David's **high priest**. Based in Jerusalem, and including most of the leading priestly families, they had their own traditions and attempted to resist the pressure of the **Pharisees** to conform to theirs. They claimed to rely only on the Pentateuch (the first five books of the Old Testament), and denied any doctrine of a future life, particularly of the **resurrection** and other ideas associated with it, presumably because of the encouragement such beliefs gave to revolutionary movements. No writings from the Sadducees have survived, unless the apocryphal book of Ben-Sirach ('Ecclesiasticus') comes from them. The Sadducees themselves did not survive the destruction of Jerusalem and the **Temple** in AD 70.

the satan, 'the accuser', demons

The Bible is never very precise about the identity of the figure known as 'the satan'. The Hebrew word means 'the accuser', and at times the satan seems to be a member of YHWH's heavenly council, with special responsibility as director of prosecutions (1 Chronicles 21.1; Job 1—2; Zechariah 3.1f.). However, it becomes identified variously with the serpent of the garden of Eden (Genesis 3.1–15) and with the rebellious daystar cast out of **heaven** (Isaiah 14.12–15), and was seen by many Jews as the quasi-personal source of evil standing behind both human wickedness and large-scale injustice, sometimes operating through semi-independent 'demons'. By Jesus' time various words were used to denote this figure, including Beelzebul/b (lit. 'Lord of the flies') and simply 'the evil one'; Jesus warned his followers against the deceits this figure could perpetrate. His opponents accused him of being in league with the satan, but the early Christians believed that Jesus in fact defeated it both in his own struggles with temptation (Matthew 4; Luke 4), his exorcisms of demons, and his death (1 Corinthians 2.8; Colossians 2.15). Final victory over this ultimate enemy is thus assured (Revelation 20), though the struggle can still be fierce for Christians (Ephesians 6.10–20).

scribes

In a world where many could not write, or not very well, a trained class of writers ('scribes') performed the important function of drawing up contracts for business, marriage, etc. Many would thus be legal experts, and quite possibly

Pharisees, though being a scribe was compatible with various political and religious standpoints. The work of Christian scribes was of vital importance in copying early Christian writings, particularly the stories about Jesus.

son of David, David's son

An alternative, and infrequently used, title for **Messiah**. The messianic promises of the Old Testament often focus specifically on David's son, for example 2 Samuel 7.12–16; Psalm 89.19–37. Joseph, Mary's husband, is called 'son of David' by the angel in Matthew 1.20.

son of God

Originally a title for Israel (Exodus 4.22) and the Davidic king (Psalm 2.7); also used of ancient angelic figures (Genesis 6.2). By the New Testament period it was already used as a **messianic** title, for example in the **Dead Sea Scrolls**. There, and when used of Jesus in the **gospels** (e.g. Matthew 16.16), it means, or reinforces, 'Messiah', without the later significance of 'divine'. However, already in Paul the transition to the fuller meaning (one who was already equal with God and was sent by him to become human and to become Messiah) is apparent, without loss of the meaning 'Messiah' itself (e.g. Galatians 4.4).

son of man

In Hebrew or Aramaic, this simply means 'mortal' or 'human being'; in later Judaism, it is sometimes used to mean 'I' or 'someone like me'. In the New Testament the phrase is frequently linked to Daniel 7.13, where 'one like a son of man' is brought on the clouds of **heaven** to 'the Ancient of Days', being vindicated after a period of suffering, and is given kingly power. Though Daniel 7 itself interprets this as code for 'the people of the saints of the Most High', by the first century some Jews understood it as a **messianic** promise. Jesus developed this in his own way in certain key sayings which are best understood as promises that God would vindicate him, and judge those who had opposed him, after his own suffering (e.g. Mark 14.62). Jesus was thus able to use the phrase as a cryptic self-designation, hinting at his coming suffering, his vindication and his God-given authority.

soul, *see* life

spirit, *see* life, holy spirit

Temple

The Temple in Jerusalem was planned by David (*c.* 1000 BC) and built by his son Solomon as the central sanctuary for all Israel. After reforms under Hezekiah and Josiah in the seventh century BC, it was destroyed by Babylon in 587 BC. Rebuilding by the returned **exiles** began in 538 BC, and was completed in 516, initiating the 'second Temple period'. Judas Maccabaeus cleansed it in 164 BC after its desecration by Antiochus Epiphanes (167). Herod the Great began to rebuild and beautify it in 19 BC; the work was completed in AD 63. The Temple was destroyed by the Romans in AD 70. Many Jews believed it should and would be rebuilt; some still do. The Temple was not only the place of **sacrifice**; it was believed to be the unique dwelling of YHWH on earth, the place where **heaven** and earth met.

Torah, Jewish law

'Torah', narrowly conceived, consists of the first five books of the Old Testament, the 'five books of Moses' or 'Pentateuch'. (These contain much law, but also much narrative.) It can also be used for the whole Old Testament scriptures, though strictly these are the 'law, prophets and writings'. In a broader sense, it refers to the whole developing corpus of Jewish legal tradition, written and oral; the oral Torah was initially codified in the **Mishnah** around AD 200, with wider developments found in the two Talmuds, of Babylon and Jerusalem, codified around AD 400. Many Jews in the time of Jesus and Paul regarded the Torah as being so strongly God-given as to be almost itself, in some sense, divine; some (e.g. Ben-Sirach 24) identified it with the figure of 'Wisdom'. Doing what Torah said was not seen as a means of earning God's favour, but rather of expressing gratitude, and as a key badge of Jewish identity.

the Twelve, *see* apostle

word, *see* good news

Word

The prologue to John's gospel (1.1–18) uses Word (Greek: *logos*) in a special sense, based on the ancient Israelite view of God's Word in creation and new creation. Here the Word is Jesus, the personal presence of the God who remains other than the world. He is the one through whom creation came into being; he is the one, now, through whom it will be healed and restored.

YHWH

The ancient Israelite name for God, from at least the time of the **Exodus** (Exodus 6.2f.). It may originally have been pronounced 'Yahweh', but by the time of Jesus it was considered too holy to speak out loud, except for the **high priest** once a year in the Holy of Holies in the **Temple**. Instead, when reading scripture, pious Jews would say *Adonai*, 'Lord', marking this usage by adding the vowels of *Adonai* to the consonants of YHWH, eventually producing the hybrid 'Jehovah'. The word YHWH is formed from the verb 'to be', combining 'I am who I am', 'I will be who I will be', and perhaps 'I am because I am', emphasizing YHWH's sovereign creative power.

STUDY/REFLECTION GUIDE

This study/reflection guide is designed to help you engage the major themes in *John for Everyone, Part 1*, either as part of a small group (for a five-week study) or in a time of personal reflection.

If using the guide with a group, each group member will need a copy of the book and should read the pages indicated prior to the group session. Because every group is unique, this guide is designed to give you flexibility and choice in customizing your group experience. You may use the format outlined below or adapt it however you wish to meet the needs, interests and schedule of your particular group. (The times indicated within parentheses are merely estimates. You may move at a faster or slower pace, making adjustments as desired.)

Suggested Format: 60 minutes

Opening Prayer (3 minutes)
Icebreaker (5–7 minutes)
Biblical Content and Commentary Highlights (5 minutes)
Group Discussion/Personal Reflection (30 minutes)
Application Exercise (10 minutes)
Closing Prayer (5 minutes)

Preceding each session outline is a brief section for the group facilitator, which includes a list of the scripture texts, the main idea and suggestions for preparation/materials needed. The opening and closing prayers are intended to cover the group in prayer. Feel free to use these prayers as printed, expand them or create your own. You also may want to include prayer requests from the group in the closing prayer. The icebreaker is provided to involve every group member from the beginning of the group session, connecting with the overarching idea that the content of John is meant for *everyone*. The biblical content and commentary highlights recap the major themes, setting the stage for group discussion. Read this material aloud or summarize it for the group. The application exercise, which is intended to be done in groups of two to three people, will help you begin thinking about how God may be inviting you to apply or respond to what you've read.

If using the guide in a time of personal reflection, modify the ice-breaker as appropriate for a fun way to begin engaging the content. You may find it helpful to journal in response to some or all of the reflection questions and then choose one or more to discuss with a friend. After reflecting on the questions in the application exercise, identify one invitation you sense God extending to you personally. Write it down, journal about it or talk with God about it throughout the coming week.

SESSION 1: JOHN CHAPTERS 1 AND 2
(PAGES 1–19)

For the Group Facilitator

Scripture Texts

John 1.1–18	The Word Made Flesh
John 1.19–28	The Evidence of John
John 1.29–34	The Lamb and the Spirit
John 1.35–42	The First Disciples
John 1.43–51	Philip and Nathanael
John 2.1–12	Water into Wine
John 2.13–25	Jesus in the Temple

The Main Idea

Jesus came for everyone and shows us who the true God is.

Suggestions for Preparation/Materials Needed

- Prepare the meeting space by arranging seats in a circle, if possible, so that everyone can see one another.
- If group members do not already know one another, have name tags and pens or markers available.
- Have on hand a whiteboard or large sheet of paper with markers for writing.
- Remind group members to read John 1 and 2 before the session and to bring their copies of this book and, if desired, a Bible (optional, since the text is included in the book). You might consider having some additional Bibles in various translations on hand.

Session Outline

Opening Prayer (3 minutes)

God, you sent Jesus to be the living Word, the one who shows us who you truly are. Open the eyes of our hearts so that we may see your glory and experience your transforming love in and through Jesus as we read John's gospel. Amen.

Icebreaker (5–7 minutes)

Go around the circle asking each person to share a word or two describing Jesus (without repeating what anyone else has shared). Write the words on a whiteboard or large sheet of paper. Say: *The author writes that Jesus came to show us who God really is. How well do these words we've listed also describe your image of God – not how you 'should' view God but how you actually do?* Invite group members to respond briefly as they are comfortable doing so.

Biblical Content and Commentary Highlights (5 minutes)

John opens the first chapter of his gospel with a prologue that introduces us to Jesus as the Word of God – the one through whom all things were made; the one who, from the start, has contained life and light; the one who is bringing into being the new creation. Perhaps the most exciting announcement we find here is that Jesus came for everyone; anyone who accepts him can become a child of God (1.12). John the Baptist humbly prepared the way for Jesus, identifying him as the one who would show us who the true God is and, ultimately, be the sacrificial lamb of God who takes away the world's sin. This is the great drama of John's gospel: Jesus reveals the glory of the unseen God, bringing the life and light of heaven to earth, but the world prefers darkness to light.

Chapter 1 includes the stories of Jesus finding his first disciples (1.35–51), who were simultaneously seeking the Messiah. In their stories, we may discover that Jesus also comes to find each of us, giving us a new vocation and new name – just as Simon became Peter, the Rock. As Jesus encounters Nathanael, who is sent to him by Philip, he makes a strange reference to the story of Jacob's ladder, in which heaven and earth are opened to each other and angels are coming and going. Here we find a clue that seems to point to Jesus as the new way in which the living God will be present with God's people. When we follow Jesus, it's as if we're seeing what happens when heaven and earth are open to each other and God's presence is unmistakably with us.

After these opening stories, John gives us the first of several clues or 'signs' that will point to moments when Jesus did what he told Nathanael he would do – bring heaven to earth so that God's transforming love could break into the world. Two powerful scenes in chapter 2 – the miracle at the wedding in Cana and the cleansing of the Temple – introduce us to the major themes of the gospel story and give us hints of where it's all going. Jesus is the true Temple, the Word made flesh, the place where God's glory dwells; and his death will be the reality to which the Passover celebration points. The chapter ends with a hint about how we should respond: If we see the signs Jesus is doing, we should trust him and believe in him.

Group Discussion/Personal Reflection (30 minutes)

1. Read aloud the prologue to John's gospel (1.1–18). What does this description of Jesus as 'the Word of God' reveal about all that Jesus was and is and did? According to the author, what did John have in mind when he wrote of Jesus as God's Word?
2. How does John 1.12 speak to God's desire for all people to become children of God? How does this verse speak to you personally?
3. How did John the Baptist prepare the way for Jesus, and what attitude did this require? What can we learn from his example that can help us to be a voice pointing others to Christ today?
4. Read aloud John 1.29. What is the significance of John the Baptist's statement that Jesus is God's lamb? What evidence does the author give to support the idea that Jesus is the true Passover lamb, and what does this mean for the world?
5. What was the sign John gave as proof that Jesus is the son of God, and what did this sign indicate Jesus would do? According to the author, how would those coming for baptism from John have understood the phrase 'son of God'?
6. What speaks to you most from the stories of the first disciples, and why? Have you ever gone looking for Jesus and discovered he was looking for you? If so, share briefly about that experience.
7. Read aloud John 1.51. What are your thoughts in response to the author's comments about this strange statement of Jesus and its possible meaning?
8. What themes of the gospel story does the author highlight in the two scenes in chapter 2 – the wedding in Cana and the cleansing of the Temple? What do these stories reveal about Jesus, his mission, and our appropriate response?

Application Exercise (10 minutes)

Break into groups of two or three and discuss the following:

- Of all the content we've covered today, what is something that strongly resonates or stands out to you?
- How does it connect with your current life experience?
- How do you sense God inviting you to respond or make application in your daily life?

Closing Prayer (5 minutes)

Loving God, thank you for becoming flesh and living among us. Remind us that when we fix our eyes on Jesus and follow him, we will be witnesses to what happens when the life and love of heaven come to earth. May Jesus continually point us to your glory and goodness, transforming our hearts and lives. Amen.

SESSION 2: JOHN CHAPTERS 3 AND 4 (PAGES 19–38)

For the Group Facilitator

Scripture Texts

John 3.1–13	Jesus and Nicodemus
John 3.14–21	The Snake and the Love of God
John 3.22–36	The Bridegroom and His Friend
John 4.1–15	The Woman of Samaria
John 4.16–26	Jesus and the Woman
John 4.27–42	Sower and Reaper Rejoice Together
John 4.43–54	The Official's Son

The Main Idea

When we believe in Jesus, we receive the new life of the spirit. This new life is available to anyone who trusts Jesus and follows him.

Suggestions for Preparation/Materials Needed

- Prepare the meeting space by arranging seats in a circle, if possible, so that everyone can see one another.
- If group members do not already know one another, have name tags and pens or markers available.

- Have on hand a whiteboard or large sheet of paper with markers for writing.
- Remind group members to read John 3 and 4 before the session and to bring their copies of this book and, if desired, a Bible (optional, since the text is included in the book). You might consider having some additional Bibles in various translations on hand.

Session Outline

Opening Prayer (3 minutes)

Jesus, you are the Word made flesh who gives us new life through the spirit. Open our hearts and minds as we read your word so that we may cultivate genuine faith that believes without seeing. Amen.

Icebreaker (5–7 minutes)

Say: *An old saying suggests that 'seeing is believing'.* As you are speaking, write this saying on a board or large sheet of paper. Go around the circle, asking each person to name a time when he or she needed to see something to believe it. Then say: *Genuine faith flips this saying like this: 'believing is seeing'.* As you are speaking, write this phrase below the first saying. Now invite group members to name things that nurture this kind of faith in us, writing their responses on the board or paper for discussion later.

Biblical Content and Commentary Highlights (5 minutes)

Chapters 3 and 4 in John's gospel focus on new life through belief in Jesus, the Word of God made flesh.

In chapter 3, Jesus tells the Pharisee Nicodemus that we must be born from above – by water and the spirit. This double-sided new birth brings us into the visible community of Jesus' followers (water baptism) and gives us new life within (spirit baptism). Jesus explains that just as Moses lifted up the bronze serpent in the wilderness and those who looked at it were saved, so those who look to the son of man who would be lifted up (on a cross) will be saved through believing in him. John looks back to chapter 1 (verses 1–2, 18) to say that Jesus was the full display of God's love. Our part is to look to Jesus and trust in God's saving love. Not believing in Jesus means remaining in darkness, and darkness must be condemned because evil destroys the present world and prevents people from coming into God's new world. The good news is that we don't have to be condemned but can believe and live. The chapter ends with John the Baptist telling his disciples that Jesus, the bridegroom, must increase, and he must decrease. John shows us

136

that what counts is not comparing ourselves with others but simply following Jesus, the Messiah, who would make Israel his bride.

In chapter 4, we find two stories. The first is of the Samaritan woman's encounter with Jesus at Jacob's Well, which reveals that Jesus is the living water that brings new life to anyone – regardless of gender, geography, or racial or moral background. The Samaritan woman believed, and she became the first evangelist to her people, many of whom recognized Jesus as saviour. This story shows us that salvation may be from the Jews, but salvation is designed to reach outside Judaism to embrace the world. Jesus went on from Samaria to Galilee, where he healed the Capernaum official's son long-distance from Cana. John points out that this second miracle in Cana is the second sign Jesus performed, and through the rest of his gospel, John will let us do our own counting of signs. Unlike the official who believed the word Jesus spoke before seeing the miracle, the Galileans wanted to see miracles before believing. The distinction between believing because we've seen something and believing on the strength of Jesus' words will remain important throughout the gospel. Genuine faith is believing in the Word become flesh, Jesus, and the result of our relationship with him is learning to love the God who so loved us (3.16).

Group Discussion/Personal Reflection (30 minutes)

1. Read aloud John 3.1–13. How would you explain what it means to be born 'from above'? How is this birth 'double-sided,' and why is this significant? How do these words of Jesus shed light on who is eligible for membership in God's kingdom?

2. Do you believe that it's more important to nurture what God is doing in the present moment than to continually think about what happened at the moment of spiritual birth? Why or why not? What are the signs of new life in your current walk with God?

3. Read aloud Numbers 21.5–8, followed by John 3.14–21. What is the connection between these two passages? How is the crucifixion of Jesus like the bronze snake on a pole? What must we do to receive the healing of God's saving love?

4. In John 3.22–36, John the Baptist refers to Jesus as the bridegroom, saying that Jesus must increase and he must decrease. What is the significance of the bridegroom reference, and what do John's comments teach us? What are your thoughts in response to C. S. Lewis's remark that we are to play great parts without pride and small parts without shame?

5. Review the author's comments regarding John 3.31–36, which is likely the gospel writer's comment on the whole chapter so far (pages 26–27). What can we learn from this contrast of 'the one from above'

137

and 'the one from the earth'? Who is competing with Jesus and the church for the ears, minds and hearts of people today? How can we know if a message has the breath, or life, of heaven?

6. Review the story of Jesus and the Samaritan woman at the well in John 4. What are three things in the story that people of that time would have found odd or problematic (pages 29–30)? What does this say about Jesus and the kingdom of God?

7. According to the author, what did 'living water' mean to the people of Jesus' day (page 30)? What does Jesus mean when he talks of living water? What insights do we find in John 7.37–39?

8. Read the conversation between Jesus and the Samaritan woman in John 4.16–26. How did Jesus cut straight to the heart of what was going on with the woman, and how did she respond? Why do you think she changed the subject? (See the author's comments on pages 31–33.) How do we see salvation beginning to embrace the world in the ending of this story (4.27–42)? What clue tells us that Jesus is excited about this development? How are you involved in 'gathering the harvest', and what emotions does this raise in you?

9. Considering that the Samaritan woman was the first evangelist, how might we define evangelism based on her example?

10. Read aloud John 4.43–54. How did the Galileans receive Jesus? Based on verse 48, would you say their faith was genuine? Why or why not? What was the second sign that Jesus performed in Cana, and what does it teach us about genuine faith?

11. What does 'believing is seeing' mean to you? Refer to the list you created during the icebreaker and discuss how each of these things helps to nurture genuine faith.

Application Exercise (10 minutes)

Break into groups of two or three and discuss the following:

- Of all the content we've covered today, what is something that strongly resonates or stands out to you?
- How does it connect with your current life experience?
- How do you sense God inviting you to respond or make application in your daily life?

Closing Prayer (5 minutes)

Jesus, we thank you for the new life you give us through the spirit and ask you to give us enthusiasm for sharing the good news of this new life with anyone and everyone who will listen. May we do your will and complete your work, always being ready to reap the harvest. Amen.

to see? Jesus' charge against them is essentially that they are reading the right book, the law of Moses, but in the wrong way (5.39–40). In other words, they know all about the hope for the Messiah yet fail to recognize him and believe.

In chapter 6, we see Jesus feeding the five thousand, walking on water, declaring himself the bread of life that comes from heaven, and sharing difficult words about eating his flesh and drinking his blood – words that cause division among his followers. The fact that these events take place at Passover has great significance. John wants us to realize that this chapter, with its stories of eating bread and walking on water, is all about the Exodus story, when God led his people through the Red Sea and fed them bread from heaven as they wandered in the wilderness. Jesus himself is the one who comes from the father to bring his people back from exile and give them new life. Though the crowd recognizes him as the prophet like Moses, the Messiah, their understanding of what that means is inadequate, as evidenced by their desire to make him king (6.14–15). Jesus wants the people to know that *he* is the bread from heaven that gives life (6.32–35). We find this statement in verse 35 – the first of the 'I am' sayings – and it's so important that Jesus repeats it in verses 48 and 51. But the people seem to be more interested in what Jesus can do for them than about who he is. The chapter ends with Jesus' difficult words about eating his flesh and drinking his blood, which have deep meaning for us related to the eucharist or Lord's supper. Jesus, the bread of life, was broken in death so that those who eat this bread of life may not die but experience the life of God's coming age. Those who partake by faith are people of the true Exodus.

Group Discussion/Personal Reflection (30 minutes)

1. Read aloud John 5.1–9a. Why did Jesus ask the man if he wanted to get well? Though the answer seems obvious, what do you think Jesus was getting at? Think of an area in your life where you desire healing. What would that healing require of you?

2. According to the author, what is significant about Jesus' words 'get up' (page 40)? How does this story of Jesus healing the man by the pool of Bethesda show us that Jesus was bringing salvation to the wider world?

3. Read aloud John 5.9b–18. Why do you think the Judeans reacted so strongly to this healing? How did Jesus' response in verse 17 make matters worse? What would it cost them to follow where the signs of Jesus were pointing? What has it cost, or required, of you?

4. How does the image of apprenticeship implied in John 5.19–23 help us to understand Jesus' relationship with the father?

5. After reading Jesus' words in John 5.24–29 about the life of God's coming age and resurrection, how would you explain these concepts to someone else? How is the miracle of resurrection already happening within those who believe, and how will it be completed in the future?

6. In what sense are Jesus' listeners 'on trial' in John 5.30–38? What evidence is Jesus pointing them to, and why? Of what are they guilty? What about us – do we *know* the God we profess to believe in? In what ways are we guilty of ignoring Jesus and living in disbelief?

7. Read aloud John 5.39–47. What charge is Jesus leveling against those who do not accept him? How had they 'been looking at the right book but reading it the wrong way' (page 49)? When are we guilty of the same charge? What does the author mean when he suggests we read the scriptures in an 'upward spiral of understanding' (page 50)?

8. Why is the detail mentioned in John 6.4 significant not only to Jesus feeding the five thousand but also to him walking on water? How is all of chapter 6 about the Exodus story, and why is this important for us to understand?

9. After Jesus fed the multitude, what was their response (6.14–15)? Based on this response, what can we discern about their understanding of who Jesus is?

10. Can you recall a time when you were in the midst of a terrible 'storm' and suddenly became aware of Jesus' presence? If so, briefly describe what that experience was like.

11. Read aloud John 6.26–35, 48, and 51. What does Jesus want the people to know about who he is? Refer to the words you wrote on the board or large sheet of paper during the icebreaker, and discuss what this first 'I am' statement of Jesus means to each of you. In what ways have you experienced Jesus as the bread of life?

12. In John 6.36–46, we find the Judaeans grumbling again. Why are they grumbling this time, and what is Jesus' response? According to the author, how do these verses echo Isaiah 54.13 and 55.1, and what do they tell us about God's initiative and our helplessness? What are those who come to Jesus promised (6.39–40, 44)?

13. In John 6.47–59 we find some of the most challenging words of Jesus. According to the author, how does the story of David in 2 Samuel 23.13–17 shed light on the deep meaning of Jesus' words (page 60–61)? What other help does the author offer us for understanding these verses (pages 61–63)? How did Jesus' words cause division among his followers (6.60–71)? What is your own response – can you relate to Peter's statement in 6.68–69?

Application Exercise (10 minutes)

Break into groups of two or three and discuss the following:

- Of all the content we've covered today, what is something that strongly resonates or stands out to you?
- How does it connect with your current life experience?
- How do you sense God inviting you to respond or make application in your daily life?

Closing Prayer (5 minutes)

Jesus, we acknowledge you as the bread of life broken in death so that we may partake of you and not die but experience the life of God's coming age. Help us to live with full awareness that this resurrection life is ours in the present, changing how we live now, as well as our hope for the life that is to come. We thank you for this inexpressible gift. Amen.

SESSION 4: JOHN CHAPTERS 7 AND 8 (PAGES 66–93)

For the Group Facilitator

Scripture Texts

John 7.1–9	Jesus and His Brothers
John 7.10–18	Disputes about Jesus
John 7.19–30	Moses and the Messiah
John 7.31–39	Rivers of Living Water
John 7.40–52	Where Does the Messiah Come From?
John 7.53–8.11	Adultery and Hypocrisy
John 8.12–20	The Light of the World
John 8.21–29	From Below or from Above
John 8.30–36	The Truth Will Make You Free
John 8.37–47	Children of Abraham – or of the Devil
John 8.48–59	Before Abraham, 'I Am'

The Main Idea

Jesus is the light of the world that shines in the darkness. If we will hear and receive his words, we will know the truth that sets us free from the slavery of sin. The all-important question remains: *Who do we believe Jesus is?*

Suggestions for Preparation/Materials Needed

- Prepare the meeting space by arranging seats in a circle, if possible, so that everyone can see one another.
- If group members do not already know one another, have name tags and pens or markers available.
- Have on hand a whiteboard or large sheet of paper with markers for writing.
- Remind group members to read John 7 and 8 before the session and to bring their copies of this book and, if desired, a Bible (optional, since the text is included in the book). You might consider having some additional Bibles in various translations on hand.

Session Outline

Opening Prayer (3 minutes)

Jesus, thank you for shining your light into our darkness. Open our hearts and minds today so that we may fully embrace who you are, receive your words of truth, and be set free from anything that would seek to separate us from you. Amen.

Icebreaker (5–7 minutes)

Say: *In the synoptic gospels of Matthew, Mark and Luke, Jesus asks his disciples, 'Who do you say that I am?'* (Matthew 16.15, Mark 8.29, Luke 9.20). *Though John's gospel does not include this encounter with Jesus and his disciples, we might say that the entire gospel points us to that question. How would you respond if someone close to you were to ask you the question,* Who is Jesus to you? Go around the circle, allowing each person to give a brief answer. Then go around the circle again, asking each person to complete the following sentence: *When I think of the many ways Jesus has set me free, I'm most grateful for . . .* Write their responses on a board or large sheet of paper for reference during the closing prayer.

Biblical Content and Commentary Highlights (5 minutes)

Chapter 7 takes us to Jerusalem for the festival of Tabernacles, or 'Booths'. Jesus' brothers want him to go with them so that he might gain a larger following, but because his 'time' has not yet come (7.6) – a time that, as John wants us to realize, points not to Tabernacles but to Passover, when the lamb will be sacrificed – Jesus follows behind them secretly. There is much dispute about Jesus among the crowds at the festival, with some approving of him and others saying he is a deceiver. The key question is whether Jesus is from God or is acting on his own authority. Halfway through the festival Jesus goes to the Temple and begins to preach, saying that his teaching comes from God and insinuating that perhaps the Judaeans cannot see it because they have closed their minds against what God wants from them. Though his brothers want him to build his own reputation, Jesus wants to boost God's reputation and provide a remedy for the problem of sin that has infected the whole world.

As Jesus continues speaking in the Temple, he raises the question of the purpose of the law, which was not to stop people from doing things but to enable them to do and be what God intended them to do and be. Beneath his words is the charge that the Judaeans are using certain aspects of the law to assure themselves that they are God's people while breaking other aspects of the law. (Specifically, they are insisting on keeping the sabbath law while being ready to kill him.) The reaction is mixed, with some saying Jesus has a demon and others wondering if he is the Messiah – though they hesitate to believe because of where he is from. Jesus responds by implying that their lack of understanding is not about him but about God. They cannot associate Jesus with the true God since they do not even know God. Even so, some do believe, and on the last day of the festival, Jesus proclaims that 'anyone who believes in him will have rivers of living water flowing out of their heart' (7.38), echoing Isaiah 55.1 and evoking Ezekiel 47. The chapter ends with some of the Pharisees sending servants to arrest Jesus and becoming angry when no one lays a hand on him. Nicodemus, the only one to speak up, reminds his fellow Pharisees that they are condemning Jesus without having heard what he has to say for himself.

Chapter 8 begins with the scribes and Pharisees wanting to stone a woman caught in adultery. Though the earliest copies of John's gospel omit this story and others place it at the end of the gospel, the story makes an important point: forgiveness means that sin matters but that God is choosing to set it aside. The rest of the chapter will make it clear that the sin that matters even more is using God's law to make oneself seem righteous, rather than allowing sin to shine the light of God's judgment into the dark places of the heart. When Jesus says that he is the light of the world (8.12), the Pharisees address his claims with a legal point, saying it is invalid for him to give evidence about himself. In response, Jesus claims his evidence is backed up by the father who sent him, giving him the two witnesses required by the law. Though Jesus and his father are giving evidence that he is the Messiah, many of his own people do not recognize him as having come from the one true God. Later Jesus addresses the Judaeans who do believe in him, saying that if they remain in his word, they will know the truth and be set free (8.32). Yet surprisingly, the people argue that, as Abraham's children, they have always been free. Jesus indicates that the children of Abraham, like the rest of the world, have been enslaved by sin, and their hope of freedom is to hear and receive his words. When Jesus refers to the Judaeans as children of the devil who are eager to carry out his murderous desires (8.44), the dialogue intensifies, leading to Jesus' bold declaration, 'Before Abraham existed, I Am' (8.58). The angry crowd accuses him of blasphemy and threatens to stone him. Bookended by violent mobs intent on stoning, this chapter highlights the darkness of the Judaeans' hearts and thinking.

Group Discussion/Personal Reflection (30 minutes)

1. What is the primary argument or dispute among the people in Jerusalem regarding Jesus? What does Jesus himself have to say about it in John 7.16–17? According to Jesus, when does it become clear to someone that he really is from God? What does the author say is the challenge for us within these words of Jesus (page 70)?

2. How was Jesus' agenda different from that of his brothers? According to the author, what is the outward sign that the church is seeking not its own glory but the glory of the one who has called and sent it (page 71)? Based on this criterion, how well would you say that we, the church, are doing at glorifying God today? Explain your response.

3. Read aloud John 7.19–30. What point is Jesus making about the law in these verses? What is the charge against the Judaeans beneath Jesus' words? How do we do something similar today, picking and choosing certain behaviors or practices to validate ourselves as 'good Christians' while ignoring others?

4. According to John 7.27, what was hindering some from fully believing in Jesus? Why was this an issue for them? Today, how do we draw wrong conclusions about Jesus based on faulty ideas of God and the world? How might we learn afresh who God is, what the world is, and who we ourselves are by looking at Jesus? What would it mean for us within the church to do this?

5. According to the author, what do Jesus' words in John 7.37–39 have to do with Isaiah 55.1 and Ezekiel 47? What is Jesus speaking about here, and why is it significant that he does so on the last day of the festival of Tabernacles? (pages 74–75)

6. In John 7.40–52 we see more division among the people about who Jesus is. What point is used again as a reason for doubt? Why do you think John doesn't address Jesus' birthplace (as do Matthew and Luke) but, instead, focuses on the servants and priests? What do Nicodemus's words in verse 51 suggest to you about where he might be in his own journey to belief in Jesus?

7. Chapter 8 contains some of the harshest things Jesus is ever recorded as saying. How might we misread the chapter if we think of the Judaeans as simply interested bystanders? What is really going on here? What is at the heart of the Judaeans' attitude?
8. How is the story of the woman caught in adultery a trap for Jesus? How did Jesus outsmart the scribes and Pharisees without minimizing sin? What does the story teach us about forgiveness?
9. What does Jesus declare about himself in John 8.12? What legal point do the Pharisees use to take issue with Jesus' claim, and how does he respond? What is Jesus revealing about them (8.19)? According to the author, how does this highlight the problem that runs throughout the chapter (page 83)?
10. Read aloud John 8.31–36. To whom is Jesus speaking here? What does he tell them, and how do they respond? What point does Jesus make in verses 34–36? What assumption had the children of Abraham made, and what was the truth that could set them free? When and how do we make a similar mistake today?
11. Toward the end of chapter 8, how does the exchange between the Judaeans and Jesus become heated? What does Jesus accuse them of, and how do they respond? What bold declaration does Jesus make in verse 58, and why does this incite the Judaeans to want to stone him?
12. What is the point Jesus has been making throughout chapter 8? What do the opening and closing scenes of the chapter tell us about the Judaeans' hearts?

Application Exercise (10 minutes)

Break into groups of two or three and discuss the following:

- Of all the content we've covered today, what is something that strongly resonates or stands out to you?
- How does it connect with your current life experience?
- How do you sense God inviting you to respond or make application in your daily life?

Closing Prayer (5 minutes)

Jesus, you are the light and the truth that set us free from the darkness of sin. Though once we were slaves to sin, now we are sons and daughters of God – true members of your family. We are so grateful for the many, many ways you have set each of us free. Today we give you thanks for delivering us from ... (*refer to the board or paper, naming each of the things you listed during the icebreaker*). May our response be to live out your sacrificial love for God and the world so that God will be glorified. Amen.

SESSION 5: JOHN CHAPTERS 9 AND 10
(PAGES 93–115)
For the Group Facilitator

Scripture Texts

John 9.1–12	The Man Born Blind
John 9.13–23	The Blind Man's Parents
John 9.24–34	Is Jesus from God?
John 9.35–41	Seeing and Not Seeing
John 10.1–10	The Good Shepherd
John 10.11–18	The Shepherd and the Sheep
John 10.19–30	The Messiah and the Father
John 10.31–42	Blasphemy!

The Main Idea

Jesus, the good shepherd, is one with the father. When we see what he is doing and hear what he is saying, we are drawn to him by the compelling power of his love.

Suggestions for Preparation/Materials Needed

- Prepare the meeting space by arranging seats in a circle, if possible, so that everyone can see one another.
- If group members do not already know one another, have name tags and pens or markers available.
- Have on hand a whiteboard or large sheet of paper with markers for writing.
- Remind group members to read John 9 and 10 before the session and to bring their copies of this book and, if desired, a Bible (optional, since the text is included in the book). You might consider having some additional Bibles in various translations on hand.

Session Outline

Opening Prayer (3 minutes)

Loving God, thank you for sending Jesus to bring light and life in this dark world. When we are surrounded by fear and doubt, help us to glimpse whatever we can of Jesus – every sign of his love that we can see and hear – so that we may follow him out of the dark into the light. Open our hearts and minds as we read your word so that we may become more aware of how he is at work in us and in our world. Amen.

Icebreaker (5–7 minutes)

Make two columns on a board or large sheet of paper, labeling one 'Seen' and the other 'Heard'. Say: *Jesus said, 'I am the good shepherd. I know my own sheep, and my own know me. . . . And I lay down my life for the sheep' (John 10.14–15). Our word 'good' can sound moralistic. But the word used here can also mean 'beautiful', as in attractive or compelling. How have you seen and/or heard the compelling love of Jesus in action, drawing you to him? You might think of a recent everyday example; a life-changing moment from the past, such as a healing or a conversion experience; or a story from the Bible.* Go around the circle, asking each person to share one or two brief examples of the compelling love of Jesus. As they share, write their responses in the appropriate columns for discussion later.

Biblical Content and Commentary Highlights (5 minutes)

The story of the man born blind in chapter 9 dismantles the idea that the world is like a moral slot machine, where we put in a coin (a good or evil act) and get out a particular result (a reward or punishment). Though there are consequences to our actions, good things do not always result from good actions, and bad things do not always result from bad actions. In saying that the man's blindness was not caused by either his or his parents' sin, Jesus is pointing to something more mysterious and hopeful going on here. The chaos of this world seems to be the raw material that God is using to make a new creation – and as John's gospel reveals, a time is coming when God will make all things new. The Pharisees and the blind man's parents demonstrate fear in the face of this mysterious healing that threatens the status quo, but the man allows Jesus' actions and words to move him from the belief that Jesus is a prophet to confident faith that he is the son of man, the Messiah. Like this man, we can follow the evidence of what Jesus has done and said toward the light of the life-giving God.

Chapter 10 begins with a parable about sheep and a shepherd. Following the previous chapter's focus on the question of whether Jesus was from God, this parable makes sense only if we understand that in the Bible the ideal king is pictured as a shepherd, signifying the intimate contact and trust between shepherd and sheep. Jesus was pointing out the difference between true shepherds and false ones to show how to recognize God's true, appointed king. The sign of the real king is the response that comes from the heart when people hear his voice and follow him out of love and trust. Because the people didn't understand this, Jesus went on to explain that the true shepherd would lie down in the gateway to protect the sheep, being willing even to die for them. If the sheep were in danger, the shepherd would take on himself the fate that otherwise would befall the sheep – which we know in Jesus' case would mean death on a cross. Jesus also spoke of enlarging the flock by bringing in different sheep, meaning the Gentiles who would come to believe in him.

Behind all this talk of sheep and shepherds is the prophecy of Ezekiel 34, which speaks of God being the true shepherd of Israel – and of David, or the Messiah, being the true shepherd. Only in Jesus can both be true. As Jesus says in verse 30, 'I and the father are one'. God is the shepherd, and Jesus, the Messiah, is the shepherd. This explains why Jesus refers to himself as the 'good' shepherd, using a word that also means *beautiful* or *attractive* – as in *compelling*. What Jesus does and says as the good shepherd draws people to himself; and when they realize he has died for them, they want even more to follow him.

Group Discussion/Personal Reflection (30 minutes)

1. Have you ever caught yourself thinking that something that seems 'unfair' must be a punishment for something you or someone else did wrong? What assumptions lie behind this kind of thinking? What can we learn from the story in John 9?
2. What were the Pharisees in this story afraid of? What were the blind man's parents afraid of? How does this story speak to many dark places in our world and lives today – places of fear, doubt, anger, resentment and anxiety? What does the author mean by suggesting that the way out of the dark and into the light is to 'glimpse whatever we can see of Jesus' (page 139)?
3. Though the man's accusers declared him sinful and threw him out of the synagogue, Jesus found him and spoke to him again. Read aloud John 9.35–39. What happened? How do we know the man was compelled to follow where the truth led him? What helps *you* to see where God is at work in a difficult situation or circumstance?
4. Have others ever tried to interpret your experience of God for you? If so, what do you know to be true about what God has done for you, and how can you hold fast to what you have seen and heard?
5. How should we respond to those who resist the light and choose to remain in darkness, even when they declare boldly that they see clearly?

6. Why does Jesus tell a parable about sheep and a shepherd at the beginning of chapter 10 (verses 1–5)? What was he trying to communicate to his listeners? According to the parable, what is the sign of God's true, appointed king? What helps you to hear and know Jesus' voice?

7. When his listeners do not understand, what further explanation does Jesus offer in John 10.7–18? How can we tell the difference between the true shepherd and the false one? How does the true shepherd keep the sheep safe, and what does this tell us about God's anointed one?

8. According to John 10.16, what else would the shepherd do for the flock? Who are the original sheep, and who are the 'other' sheep?

9. According to the author, how do we see the ancient prophecy of Ezekiel 34 in these verses about the shepherd and sheep in John 10 (page 109)? How does verse 30 shed light on the seeming dichotomy of the prophecy – that both God and the Messiah are the shepherd?

10. How does our typical understanding of 'good shepherd' differ from what Jesus meant when he spoke of himself this way in John 10.11, 14? How was Jesus' meaning controversial and even dangerous? (See the author's comments on pages 108–9.)

11. In John 10.19–30, we return to the question of whether Jesus is the Messiah (verse 24). If Jesus has not said, in so many words, that he is the Messiah, why does he say that he told them and they didn't believe? To what is he referring? And how does the rest of the chapter point to the same evidence?

12. What promise does Jesus make in John 10.28, and what is his guarantee for this claim (10.29–30)? How do the Judaeans respond to Jesus' statements (10.31–33)? What do his words evoke within you?

13. Read aloud John 10.37–38. What is Jesus' argument and plea? Now refer to the list created during the icebreaker. When you look to the works of Jesus in the Bible and in our lives today, what is your response?

Application Exercise (10 minutes)

Break into groups of two or three and discuss the following:

- Of all the content we've covered today, what is something that strongly resonates or stands out to you?
- How does it connect with your current life experience?
- How do you sense God inviting you to respond or make application in your daily life?

Closing Prayer (5 minutes)

Thank you, Jesus, for opening our eyes so that we may see. Thank you for teaching us to hear and know your voice. Good shepherd, continue leading us toward your beautiful light so that it may heal, direct and protect our lives as we follow you in love and trust. Amen.